Walter Lippmann and His Times

Walter Lippmann

AND HIS TIMES

Edited by Marquis Childs and James Reston

Harcourt, Brace and Company ⊞ *New York*

© 1959 by Marquis Childs and James Reston

Library of Congress Catalog Card Number: 59-10255
Printed in the United States of America

Notes on Contributors

MARQUIS CHILDS' syndicated column on politics and foreign affairs appears in 175 American newspapers. A correspondent for the St. Louis *Post-Dispatch*, he is also author of many books, including *Eisenhower: Captive Hero* and *Sweden: The Middle Way*.

CARL BINGER is a noted psychiatrist and has been a friend of Walter Lippmann since their childhood in New York and undergraduate years at Harvard. He is now a consulting psychiatrist for several colleges and hospitals around Boston, Massachusetts, and the author of several books.

GEORGE F. KENNAN, former U.S. Ambassador to the Soviet Union, is now a permanent professor of the Institute for Advanced Study in Princeton, New Jersey. He has received many awards, including a Pulitzer Prize, for the work on which he is currently engaged, several volumes on *Soviet-American Relations 1917-20*.

ALLAN NEVINS, historian and teacher recently retired from Columbia University, spent much of the first twenty years of his career on the editorial staffs of the New York *Evening Post*, the *Nation*, the New York *Sun*, and the New York *World*. Author and editor of many books of American history and biography, he is associated with the Huntington Library in California.

ARTHUR KROCK, Washington commentator for the New York *Times*, has been analyzing politics for the *Times* since 1927, when he joined its staff. His work in Washington has twice brought him a Pulitzer Prize for his commentary on the political scene.

RAYMOND ARON, columnist for *Le Figaro*, is France's leading journalist and political analyst and a professor at the Sorbonne and at the Institut d'Etudes Politiques. His books on world affairs include *Century of Total War* and *Opium of the Intellectuals*.

IVERACH McDONALD has been the foreign editor of the *Times* of London since 1952. As editor and correspondent for that paper for many years, he has traveled extensively and has covered major international conferences since World War II.

FRANK MORAES, one of the foremost journalists of India, has been the editor of the *Indian Express* of Bombay. His books include *Jawaharlal Nehru, a Biography, Report on Mao's China*, and *Yonder One World: A Study of Asia and the West*.

HARRY S. ASHMORE, the editor of the *Arkansas Gazette* of Little Rock, Arkansas, won two Pulitzer Prizes last year for his outstanding courage in reporting the integration crisis. He is the author of *Epitaph for Dixie* and other books on the South.

REINHOLD NIEBUHR, theologian and philosopher, is professor of applied Christianity at Union Theological Seminary in New York City. Dr. Niebuhr has written many books interrelating religion, morals, government, and history, including *Moral Man and Immoral Society*, *The Children of Light and the Children of Darkness*, and *The Self and the Dramas of History*.

ARTHUR M. SCHLESINGER, JR., is professor of history at Harvard University, specializing in American intellectual history. He was one of the founders of ADA and aided in the Democratic presidential campaigns of 1952 and 1956. Currently at work on *The Age of Roosevelt*, he received a Pulitzer Prize in 1945 for *The Age of Jackson*.

JAMES RESTON, chief of the Washington Bureau of the New York *Times* since 1953, has been with the *Times* for twenty years. During that period, he has won many awards, including two Pulitzer Prizes, for his reporting and analysis of national and international news.

Contents

ix

CONTENTS

I

Introduction: The Conscience of the Critic

BY MARQUIS CHILDS

For nearly fifty years Walter Lippmann has been a critic of the politics, the morals, the manners of the world around him. Through this extraordinary span, when the very fabric of Western civilization was being strained to the breaking point, he has kept a clear and steady vision. If, as his accusers have said, he has from time to time descended into mere urbanity, what must be wondered at in such a long career devoted to the public philosophy is that the level was so often so high.

Inevitably, he has drawn his share of scorn in these years. As he has risen to eminence, this has been the kind of scorn reserved for the closet or a corner of the cocktail party. At least two Secretaries of State have gnashed their teeth, calling down imprecations on one who preferred thinking to doing, and who in thinking ventured to criticize and even at times to castigate the doers. For, while we respect our thinkers, we are happier when they confine themselves to the realm of pure thought. During the era of the New Deal, when not to be for the brave new world was to be against it, old friends broke crossly with a critic who persisted in being critical. The intolerable affront was that one so obviously of a liberal and humane view should not subscribe with all his heart to the effort to remake the old order.

To have escaped the pitfalls of partisanship, whether of person or of party, is for Lippmann, now that he has reached the age of seventy, no small part of his triumph. The sad wreckage of those who have been less fortunate is strewn all around. Having undertaken the role of critic, they found themselves following in the train of this or that great man or this or that ideology or party. The end was almost bound to be disillusion and revulsion. We have seen the venom of these former partisans, their fury at the false god, whether of left or right or middle, who betrayed them. The rancor of their cries fills the air, not infrequently to the exclusion of rational discussion.

The essays in this book are an examination of various phases of the career of a critic who, more than any other American today, has achieved through his pen a worldwide audience. While they find fault with certain phases of his career, they are written with respect for the clarity and the penetration of his vision and the objectivity of judgment that has come from that vision. It is the phenomenon of the thinking man and the influence he has exerted on his times.

Walter Lippmann's career divides itself into three separate and more or less distinct phases. He was first the precocious young intellectual in whom everyone saw an infinite promise. The impression he gave, and this has been true throughout his life, was of one singularly blessed by fortune. His eager, searching mind had impressed not only his contemporaries in his class at Harvard, a class starred by an exceptional number of brilliant young men, but George Santayana and William James and others of the great teachers who were then in Cambridge. One of his classmates and friends was John Reed. Another was T. S. Eliot. Having completed the work for his degree in three years, he served as assistant to Santayana in his fourth year, and left Harvard with his class in 1910, when he was twenty-one.

He was handsome and self-contained almost to the point of aloofness, but his youthful idealism nevertheless shone through. He had joined the Harvard Socialist Club, and much of his writing in undergraduate publications dealt with social change and the inevitability of reform. It was an age of innocence, a cheerful kind of false dawn, in which everything seemed possible by the exercise of a modicum of reason. William James was its prophet on one level and H. G. Wells on another and more popular level. The brilliant young intellectual just out of Harvard found so much that was wrong in the world around him, yet he seems never to have doubted that the means to right those wrongs were ready and waiting, if human beings would only follow the course of reason. Lincoln Steffens discovered him shortly after his fourth year at Harvard, and he joined the staff of *Everybody's Magazine*.

A year and a half later, on January 1, 1912, he became executive secretary to the new Socialist mayor of Schenectady, the Reverend George R. Lunn. During this brief adventure he discovered two things: first, that he had no taste whatsoever for practical politics and, second, that people who voted Socialist and who called themselves Socialists knew little or nothing of what Socialism meant.

With this characteristic discovery of the intellectual, he resigned at the end of four months. The urgent need was to educate the people to the meaning of Socialism. There seems to have been in his Socialism at this time little of the orthodoxy of Marxism. It was the Socialism of reform —the reforms of the day, conservation, slum clearance, woman's suffrage. But at the same time, he was impatient with the temporizing of those who seemed to believe that by tinkering and patching after enough successes at the polls, the Socialist millennium could be achieved. In short, his was the position of the intellectual, the critic, for whom the tiresome and often dubious necessities of political life were distasteful. In his first book, *A Preface to Politics*, published in 1913, he still flirted with the Socialism of reform. But the following year, in *Drift and Mastery*, he rejected the Socialist movement as an exercise in doctrinaire sterility, with Marx an empty prophet.

An intellectual adventure full of large excitement, characteristic of the innocent hope of these years just before the catastrophe of the war, had come to absorb him. Herbert Croly had invited him to become one of the board of editors of the *New Republic*. This new weekly set out to ruffle the calm assumptions of an America content and complacent in the interval that followed Theodore Roosevelt and his excursion into empire. In his book *The Promise of American Life*, Croly had given form to the ideals of those who saw a generous, liberal America setting an example for the world, a promise not in pride of place or design of power, but in a full realization of the potentialities of freedom for the individual, potentialities as yet only dimly perceived. He had obtained the backing of Willard Straight and Straight's charming and intelligent

4

wife, the former Dorothy Whitney. Although they supplied the financial backing, the Straights were to have
only one voice on the editorial board and that voice of no
greater authority than the word of the other editors. This
was splendid idealism bent on a high editorial goal. For
the first issue, Lippmann wrote a review of H. G. Wells's
The Wife of Sir Isaac Harman.

That first number appeared on November 7, 1914.
While they could have only a dim comprehension of it,
the comfortable shape of the world as those idealistic
young men had known it was already cracked, and a chain
of consequences set in motion the terror and despair of
which we have not yet known in full measure. Lippmann
has told in *U.S. Foreign Policy,* published in 1943, how he
sailed for England in June of 1914, a few days after the
assassination of Archduke Ferdinand in Sarajevo. He had
a pleasant time in London, bicycled through the lake
country, attended a gathering of Fabian socialists presided
over by Sidney and Beatrice Webb and Bernard Shaw, and
then crossed to Belgium in the last week of July and
bought a ticket for a journey through Germany on his way
to Switzerland, where he intended to take a walking tour
in the Alps. He recalls being astonished and even a little
annoyed when he went to the railway station and found
the German border closed because Belgium had received
an ultimatum from Germany. Not until he returned to
England and by chance was in the lobby of the House of
Commons on August 4, 1914, the day war was declared,
he confessed, did he begin to take foreign affairs seriously.

Both Lippmann and the *New Republic* were soon
caught up in the drama of the war and the threat to
America's determined neutrality. *The Stakes of Diplo-*

macy, which appeared in 1915, was a remarkably clear-sighted analysis of the causes of the war and the perils certain to persist even after it was concluded. Written when he was twenty-five, it showed the quality that was to win him such a wide and respectful audience in later years: the ability to grasp a set of facts, analyze them with force and clarity, and come up with a simple and cogent conclusion. While in part the book was a rationalization of America's traditional open-door policy, it was much more than this. The young author sensed that the open door to free trade and competitive commerce by the developed nations of the world in the undeveloped areas would not bring an automatic equilibrium and thereby the basis for a stable peace. He was discussing, of course, the rivalry of the French, the British, and the Germans over Morocco and the Agadir incident that had been like a lightning flash in a dark sky heralding the storm of World War I. Speaking of the horrors of the Congo, "the ravishing and despoiling and debauching of natives by the European," he went on to say that the interrelation of peoples had gone so far that to advocate international *laissez faire* was to utter a counsel of despair. What he proposed, therefore, was to internationalize or Europeanize those undeveloped areas in which friction was certain to generate. In each instance a kind of legislature made up of both Europeans and natives would direct the orderly evolution of the territory. What made his internationalism especially plausible, he wrote, was that it was not spread thin as a "parliament of man" but would be sharply limited to the sources of friction where internationalism was most obviously needed. One of the areas he discussed was China, which lay defenseless under the onslaught of the great powers that were in ruthless competition for imperial conquest. His diagnosis of the tragedy of China forty-five years ago was extraordinarily prescient and far-seeing, so much so that it might have been written in 1940 or even 1945.

"Only the blindness which does not see beyond the immediate present can feel anything but sorrow if China is on the road to chaos. For the trouble being prepared by the weakness of China will trouble the world. It will haunt its peace. And no clairvoyance is needed to prophesy that if China is unable to stand on its feet and assume control of its own affairs, innocent people the world over will pay taxes for armaments, and those who are boys today will perish on distant battle fields. This is no scaremongering. The Chinese are almost a quarter of the human race. Let them sink into helpless disorder, thwart them, oppress them, and they will become to the world what Turkey and the Balkan States have been to Europe—a running sore which infects everyone."

In the young Lippmann were many of the trends later to be confirmed and deepened. He preferred to trust the "cool intentions" of Woodrow Wilson after the sinking of the *Lusitania* rather than to risk calling Congress back into session and producing a spate of interviews, speeches, resolutions, and demands. With danger in the air and the most delicate diplomacy required, Demos must be kept on a tight leash. The President in such a situation exercised extraordinary power, power of a magnitude that the Constitution never contemplated, but there was no alternative. To our surprise and humiliation, he wrote in a revealing passage, some of us discovered that our desire for peace and our faith in democratic institutions conflicted. We had to choose between them, and if we won a peace, he confessed, it was by an abandonment of the pretense that the people could control their foreign relations in any positive way. We trusted a President who was elected before the submarine war was dreamed of, and, as it happened, he turned out to be a man who wanted to avoid war. In the Lippmann view, this was not the careful calculation of democracy, but a fortunate accident.

The discovery may help to explain why he gravitated toward President Wilson. While he has insisted that the closeness to Wilson was for the most part at second or third hand, through Colonel House, the *New Republic* and Lippmann, as one of its principal voices, seem to have exercised considerable influence on the President. One of the contributors to this volume shows the nature of the relationship and the way in which Lippmann was tempted to venture for a second time into more or less direct participation in the process of government. He became one of a group working on the background material on which Wilson was to base his Fourteen Points. After serving as an army captain in an intelligence unit on the Meuse-Argonne front, he went to Paris, where with other brilliant younger men he undertook to prepare the way for a Wilsonian peace of justice under a new world order.

But disillusion, as in the earlier and simpler venture in Schenectady, was not long in coming. He worked very hard in the cause of what he believed at the outset to be the opportunity for a noble peace. In the chaos that came with the ending of the war, so much had to be improvised. Lloyd George and Orlando wanted to know the significance of the Fourteen Points on which the Germans had conditioned their surrender. Lippmann labored for twenty-four hours continuously preparing a précis of thirteen of the points. The fourteenth point was analyzed by Frank Cobb, the editor of the New York *World*. The detailed and careful memorandum they prepared was then cabled to Wilson, who approved it for sending to the Italian and British Prime Ministers.

Wilson came to Paris at the head of the American delegation, and in the view of his young disciple this was a tragic error. The commitments the President made in this way were so final that no room was left for compromise with Congress later. Further and final disillusion came when Wilson sanctioned the use of American troops in Russia, joining with the other Allies in an attempt to curb, if not erase, the consequences of the Bolshevik revolution. To Lippmann, this seemed a tragic betrayal of the principle of self-determination. He has said that he tried in vain to remind the President of the incongruity of the situation, pointing out that by participating in a war of subjugation during the era of pacification, the Allies were bound to cancel out the effectiveness of the peace treaty they were drafting. Lippmann left Paris for America in something like despair.

His return marked the beginning of the middle phase of his career. For a brief time he resumed his work with the *New Republic*, resigning to finish the book *Public Opinion*, on which he was then working. His intellectual interests at this time were wide-ranging. Through his friend Felix Frankfurter, he was able to bring to America the rights to John Maynard Keynes's *The Economic Consequences of the Peace*. With Keynes to Lippmann's publisher, Harcourt, Brace, came most of the Bloomsbury

9

group. Not long after he left the *New Republic,* Herbert Bayard Swope, as executive editor, asked Lippmann to become a member of the editorial-page staff of the New York *World.* Croly was deeply offended. He felt that his protégé was abandoning him for the fleshpots of metropolitan journalism. That Lippmann suffered too, there seems no doubt, since beneath his reserve he is highly sensitive, with a strongly developed conscience.

Many of his admirers felt that he was betraying the idealistic promise of his youth. They may have recognized that the *World* was America's most brilliant and scintillating newspaper, on which almost any ambitious young man would have been proud to have a place. But in their eyes, and this was particularly true of Croly, Walter Lippmann had been dedicated to something more than assured success in the popular acceptance of that dubious word.

If success was what he sought, it was never in doubt. He served under the legendary Frank Cobb, one of the few editors of true greatness in American journalism, until Cobb's death in 1923, when he became editor. His position at the age of thirty-four was perhaps the most enviable in daily journalism in America. The *World* was a constellation of men, witty, brilliant, sometimes even searching and profound. Their names, Rollin Kirby, Heywood Broun, Arthur Krock, James M. Cain, Franklin P. Adams, and many others, evoke a time that today seems more distant than the Stone Age. They set the pace for the New York, which is to say the America, of the twenties. It was gay, rich, dazzling, cynical. In the midst of this lush profusion, Lippmann often seemed, to borrow a phrase applied more aptly to another figure of the era, Calvin Coolidge—a Puritan in Babylon.

10

There are widely varying views of Lippmann as editor. From firsthand knowledge, Allan Nevins appraises his editorship in this volume. The issues of the day seemed increasingly to present themselves in terms of a crude black and a violent white. The editor of the leading liberal paper in America was expected to take sides, and Lippmann was frequently unhappy at having to come down on one side or the other. He was the thinker, weighing and measuring the alternatives, rather than the partisan advocate. This was dramatized in the famous controversy with Heywood Broun, the most widely read columnist on the *World*'s famous "op. ed." page, who accused the editor of capitulating to respectability in the Sacco and Vanzetti case. While denouncing the injustice to the two Italian anarchists, the *World* praised the commission, headed by A. Lawrence Lowell, the President of Harvard, that had confirmed the guilt of the two men. Broun continued to speak out, with the wry humor and the withering irony that made him so popular, against the editorial position of his paper. The end result was his discharge, and he went to the *Telegram*.

With the stock-market crash and the beginning of the Depression, the national scene appeared even more sharply contrasted in the unrelieved black of the bad old past and the radiant white of a future to be written in accord with the innumerable prescriptions of a whole host of apostles of hope. With all values sharply accentuated and a clamor of voices rising from each side of a rapidly widening divide, the *World* found itself in a kind of limbo in which the qualities that had made it a strong and widely appealing newspaper seemed to have lost their attraction. Innumerable post-mortems have been held on the demise of the *World*, and there is no intention here to rehearse the unhappy circumstances that led to the sale of the paper. It was a tragedy marking the beginning of the gradual contraction of the newspaper business. There were to be fewer and fewer newspapers, and the degree of editorial independence seemed likewise to shrink. In a sense, it was a tragedy for Lippmann, too, or that is what many of his loyal friends felt at the time.

What astonished his friends was that the man whom they considered a convinced liberal should accept a position as columnist for the New York *Herald Tribune*. As a champion of the Republican party, the *Herald Tribune* under the Ogden Reids had continued to carry on a tradition of enlightened conservatism. It was the newspaper of Wall Street and the banking community, a defender of the tax policies of Andrew Mellon and Ogden Mills, which the *World* in its day had strongly criticized. How would Walter Lippmann fit into such an environment? This was the question raised by those who had followed his career through the years. Although the announcement by the *Herald Tribune* had said that under his contract he would have full freedom of expression as an independent columnist, skepticism prevailed. They felt he would inevitably be overwhelmed in the milieu of a strongly Republican newspaper.

In form and manner, in format and length, the column that he began to write in September of 1931 is very much the same column that he writes today. It was outwardly the same Lippmann who was to win such an extraordinary number of readers in almost every country in the world. But the resemblance between the early columnist and the columnist of today is merely superficial. Lippmann did not in those early years develop his sureness of touch, and it is to that time that his critics look to try to prove the charge of inconsistency and bad judgment. This was in many respects perhaps the most unfortunate period in his career. One reason was the curiously arbitrary nature of the judgments he passed upon Franklin D. Roosevelt. As editor of the *World*, Lippmann had been deeply immersed in the politics of New York City and New York State. Roosevelt appeared as an outsider, an interloper, who by a turn of the wheel of fortune against all the odds was elected governor of New York in 1928. He was also an amateur, and Lippmann has always had the highest respect for meticulous professionalism. His judgment of Roosevelt in January of 1932, as the presidential contest of that year drew near, has been most often held against him by those who would convict him of prejudice and political naïveté. The quotation frequently cited is from a column published on January 8: "Franklin D. Roosevelt is no crusader. He is no tribune of the people. He is no enemy of entrenched privilege. He is a pleasant man who, without any important qualifications for the office, would very much like to be President." There were in succeeding months other judgments that seem in hindsight to have been nearly as mistaken.

The explanation lies in part in the striking difference in the character of the two men. Roosevelt understood better than any politician of our time the conflicting currents of opinion, the deep underlying tides of prejudice, that make it so difficult under a system of divided powers to gain and hold the support of a working majority for any policy. With the intuitiveness of a great artist, he met each situation as it arose. For Lippmann, the intellectual, seeking a confrontation of issues in a debate of right and wrong, this was anathema. In the months leading up to the selection of a presidential candidate, Governor Roosevelt was being pressed to remove James J. Walker as mayor of New York and thereby end the scandalous regime of this playboy out of the twenties. But, since this would have alienated Tammany Hall and thereby have put the allegiance of the New York delegation to the nominating convention in jeopardy, Roosevelt was behaving with the political guile of which he was later to become a master, waiting until Walker should serve as his own executioner. Lippmann, moreover, had in Newton D. Baker, Secretary of War under Wilson, a candidate whom he preferred for the nomination. With his capacities demonstrated in the Wilson administration, Baker seemed to Lippmann a much more solid candidate.

Nevertheless, once Roosevelt was in the White House, and with the nation in the midst of the severest economic crisis in its history, Lippmann took a hopeful view of the New Deal. While in a sense he was a liberal in the classical meaning of the word, he was not beguiled, as were so many of his colleagues and contemporaries, into believing that Roosevelt was willfully imposing government collectivism on a society that had until that moment been enjoying the unalloyed freedoms of Jefferson's rural democracy. The collectivism of the great corporations had long since profoundly altered those freedoms. Lippmann understood this very well, and he had frequently addressed himself to the need to correct the imbalance of powers that had come into being under the corporate system. In *Drift and Mastery*, he argued with persuasive logic the need for strong trade unions to counterbalance the power of private industry and thereby help to promote stable industrial relations. Roosevelt, as Lippmann readily recognized, was in search of makeweights essential if the economy were to be restored to a going condition with a hope of a relatively stable balance for the future. When, however, it came to ways and means, the critic, after his first admiring respect, became increasingly suspicious of the President. So much of the New Deal seemed hastily improvised, crude, and unworkable. It was one step forward and another step back. The new agencies brought into being to cope with various aspects of the crisis were working at cross-purposes. Lippmann was increasingly alienated, and many friends out of the past who were then in Washington struggling to put the unemployed back to work and restore America's productivity found his strictures intolerable. The break was complete when, in the fall of 1936, he declared for Alfred M. Landon. To many, it appeared that the brilliant intellectual of a few years before had surrendered his vision of the future to lapse into the delusion of a conservatism that no longer had any validity whatsoever. Roosevelt's triumph in carrying all but two of the forty-eight states seemed to put the seal of final rejection on one who had once held so high the liberal banner.

What this attitude of so many of Lippmann's old friends and associates overlooked was the almost inherent necessity of the critic to criticize, to oppose whatever is. That is a strong element in Lippmann's temperament. Indeed, it may be argued that this is the function of the critic if he is to provide the insights, the illumination, that will help men to govern themselves more wisely in a free society. Rarely may he applaud or even cheer. But almost always over the years, Lippmann's function has been to raise the intellectual standard and remind fallible men trying to meet the crises of their time of the values that are timeless. It goes without saying that this is not an endearing function. When, as in the years after 1929, the doers are hard pressed to keep the wheels of mere existence turning, the role of the critic is a particularly unhappy one.

The year 1938 marked a sharp break with the past and the beginning of the third phase of Lippmann's career. Divorced from the former Faye Albertson, he married Helen Byrne Armstrong. They moved from New York to Washington to live, and soon had found a circle of new friends. Increasingly, Lippmann turned his attention to world affairs and the menacing shadow of another war. His writing took on a new immediacy and urgency, although he continued to maintain the restraint and balance that have characterized his work from the start. If the follies of the years leading up to the debacle filled him at times with despair, he put forward in his column as always the cool prescription of reason and sanity. Writing from Washington, which, with the Depression and the New Deal, had become the center of economic power and was, with the ever-darkening shadow of the oncoming war, to become increasingly a world capital, Lippmann's influence grew in both range and depth. His writing had an authority, a confidence, that it had sometimes lacked before. Where he had often leaned on others, he now trusted more and more to his own opinions. He was approaching the mature phase of the unfettered critic whose words were to be so widely read and respected. This phase is treated at length, by James Reston, in the concluding essay in this volume.

Similarly, in the war years his influence was to grow.

One of the brilliant younger men on the remarkable staff serving in the British Embassy during the war remarked that if he had his way, His Majesty's government would maintain in Washington an exceptionally able foreign-service officer with the rank of minister accredited solely to Walter Lippmann. It was a tribute to the weight that his words carried. He was sometimes critical of President Roosevelt's conduct of the war, and particularly on the score of "unconditional surrender." To Lippmann, this seemed to make impossible any conclusion of the conflict short of inflicting on Germany a punishment that would leave an ineradicable heritage of hatred and vindictiveness. As the grim doubts of the first months gave way to a certitude of victory, he was more and more concerned with the peace that should come at the end of the war. His *U.S. Foreign Policy* relates the past to the responsibilities inevitably to fall on the United States with the coming of peace. Twice, once in 1942 and again in 1944, he visited the theater of the war in England and France. He was received as a kind of special ambassador by everyone from Winston Churchill on down.

It was to be that way in the years after the war, too, as the Foreign Office and his friends in journalism and elsewhere in London arranged a schedule for his annual visitations that began with the Prime Minister, ran the gamut of the party in power, the opposition, and all shades of opinion in between. He had become a world figure. With his concentration and singleness of purpose, his refusal to be deflected by the easy distractions that are the concomitant of power and fame in America, he had put himself in the forefront of commentators and critics. While this brought him a wider and wider audience, it meant at the same time that he was the target of envy and resentment as well as the criticisms of those who sincerely felt that he husbanded his authority far too narrowly, with a caution bordering on timidity.

In 1945, Professor Fred Rodell, of the Yale Law School, writing in the *American Mercury*, directed a sharp attack against Lippmann. His thesis was one familiar to the critics of the critic. It was that he wraps in portentousness, not to say solemnity, of language ideas of small import. For the ordinary reader, the elaborateness of the package conceals the meagerness of the gift inside. What these critics ignore, of course, is the burden imposed on one who undertakes to write a column five, three, or even two times a week, as Lippmann does today. The level will necessarily be uneven. It is on his best work, and, given the pressures of day-to-day journalism, the standard is remarkably high, that he must be judged. To his task he brings a profound seriousness, a sense of dedication, that is rare. If he is disturbed by the criticism of those who call him an "appeaser," attacking him for being too ready to negotiate with the Soviet Union toward ultimate coexistence, he gives no sign of it. Outwardly, the face he presents to the world is one of serene circumspection. He and his wife live within a routine carefully and pleasantly ordered, moving from their spacious house in Washington to the quiet seclusion of their "camp" in Maine on a schedule as fixed as the seasons.

The good fortune that has marked almost every stage of Walter Lippmann's career promises to give him a long lease on posterity. A number of magazine articles have been written about Lippmann, and one slim book, *Walter Lippmann, a Study in Personal Journalism*, by David

Elliott Weingast. The last is a useful review of the Lippmann career. But from the standpoint of history, his good fortune consists in having found a compiler who with admiration as well as thoroughgoing skill collects every scrap of Lippmanniania. Robert O. Anthony is honorary curator of the Lippmann room in the library of Yale University. While at Amherst College, Anthony, now a business executive in Providence, Rhode Island, developed an admiration for the commentator which became a lifelong hobby. No other journalist and few public figures will have had a career so carefully documented for the historian of the future. In the Lippmann room are 288 articles by Walter Lippmann; 72 articles about Walter Lippmann; 122 reviews of Walter Lippmann's books; 120 portraits, photographs, caricatures, and cartoons of Walter Lippmann; ten volumes of New York *World* editorials, which Lippmann compiled, with the author of each editorial identified; and 89 volumes of his "Today and Tomorrow" column, all cross-indexed. The bibliography of his works consists of twenty-six volumes, on three of which he had collaborators, and two volumes that he edited and wrote introductions for. It includes thirty-six foreign editions of his works and 66 books about or mentioning Lippmann. This is only to suggest the wealth in the Lippmann room, which includes manuscripts, personal letters, and degrees and decorations from foreign governments conferred on the author.

It is a remarkable record of an extraordinary phenomenon which history can scarcely ignore. One can only conjecture what history may say. The voice of reason has more often than not seemed a still small voice drowned in the terrible cacophony of the monstrous events of our time. But with Lippmann it has been an unfailing voice, a sure line. Only those who have fallen into utter despair or who have found refuge in an unalloyed cynicism will deny that it may finally sound above the din of the wild and the irrational. This is the strength of Walter Lippmann, and it is the faith that he has kept for the fifty years of his writing career.

II

A Child of the Enlightenment

BY CARL BINGER

Walter Lippmann was born on September 23, 1889. Queen
Victoria was widowed but still sitting comfortably on her
throne. Her grandson, Kaiser Wilhelm II, had just acceded
to his throne, proclaiming the divine right of the House
of Hohenzollern to rule, and shortly thereafter he dismissed the Iron Chancellor, Bismarck, who was the first
chancellor of the New German Empire. Grover Cleveland
was in the White House, finishing out his first term. And
the "best people" were Republicans, though some of them
—the first mugwumps—had voted for Cleveland. These
good people lived in brownstone houses and they didn't
throw stones. The upper middle class had risen to a point
of secure, well-fed comfort. Irish and German servant
girls could be hired for twenty dollars a month. Labor
unions were not a threat to anyone's peace of mind, and
the wound of our Civil War seemed to be healing. The
Maine had not yet been sunk. Cuba and the Philippines
were still Spanish possessions, and the United States of
America had not spread its power beyond this continent.

Almost seven years to the day after his birth—that is, in late September 1896—Walter entered the primary class of Dr. Julius Sachs's School for Boys, which was situated at 32 West 59th Street in New York City, long since replaced by a towering apartment house on Central Park South. The classroom teacher was a little gray-haired lady named Miss Estvan. Walter soon became her pet. There were perhaps a dozen other little boys in her class. I was one of them, and through all the succeeding years, now sixty-three, Walter and I have been friends. What I shall have to say about him will therefore suffer the bias and distortion of friendship.

I suppose that in many respects his character was already formed before I laid eyes on him. Certainly it has been extraordinarily consistent ever since. I believe that with him, as with most of us, the plan of personality is laid down very early in life. The fact that he was an only child had, of course, much to do with his particular development. He never had to suffer the arrows of sibling rivalry. He was, moreover, from early childhood the center of interest and devotion of three adoring adults—his parents and his maternal grandmother, who lived with them. They planned for him, protected him, and watched over him. They saw to it that he had "every advantage." There was always money enough, not only for comfortable living in New York, but for travels abroad in the summers on the best steamers and visits to the best hotels. All this made him rather special—precocious, perhaps, and timid, but not "spoiled" in the usual sense of that word. In my experience, children who are spoiled are the ones who are deprived of love—not those who are given it. His grandmother, perhaps, gave him the most tenderness and companionship. She was the one to whom he remained most closely attached. His mother was a little too ambitious and worldly, but I am sure very intelligent and gifted. His father, though successful and kind, seemed, to me at least, without much color or force, and I doubt whether he served as a model for Walter.

But what made Walter special was his extraordinary intellectual capacity and discipline. This simply put him in a class by himself. I don't suppose he ever got less than an A on any examination in his life. This habit began in Miss Estvan's class in 1896 and continued until we graduated from Harvard in 1910. He could recite the names of the states and their capitals in less time than anyone else in the class. He could point out where the Guadalquivir arose and emptied and also the Guadeloupe. He knew his French irregular verbs so well that our goateed teacher, M. Jean Pierre Auguste Porret, preened himself when his prodigy of a pupil recited. He could translate Ovid at sight, to the delight of Mr. Weiberzahl, the Latin teacher, and, later, all the efforts of Mr. Douglas, whom we nicknamed "Digamma Dougy," to teach us Greek met with success with Walter only. Dr. Julius Sachs, the bearded Jehovah who presided over the school, used to tweak our ears when we flubbed our translation of Xenophon, but I doubt that Walter's ever got tweaked. Sachs retired to become Professor of Secondary Education at Columbia's Teachers College. He was succeeded by an erect, florid-faced, blond Teuton named Dr. Otto Koenig, a man of character and not without humor, who held up the standards of scholarship. He admired Lippmann greatly and expected much from him and was always proud of him.

But the two teachers who had perhaps the greatest

influence on Lippmann were the Thompson brothers, Fred and Dan. They were Amherst graduates from Augusta, Maine. They brought with them a salty Yankee quality that was a good leaven for the Old World, urban atmosphere of the school. Fred taught history, and though perhaps not a great teacher, he was a lovable character who warmed especially to Walter's alert and precise eagerness. He was also the football coach, but Walter's musically talented mother had him give up football for piano lessons. She also saw to it that he had a professional shampoo once a week. This struck us all as remarkable. Whether his still extant fine head of hair can be attributed to this early care or to the happy mozaic of genes that went into his make-up I do not know. He always had a good deal of physical vigor and enjoyed games and became a passable tennis player.

We practiced football on the Hoguet estate on Riverside Drive at about 140th Street. The Hoguet boys were at our school, and their father, Mr. Robert Hoguet, owned a fine Victorian mansion, commanding a superb view of the sweep of the Hudson. The house sat high up, with its lawns rolling down to the Drive. Across it, where the New York Central tracks now run, was our football field, and here Fred Thompson tried to make rather indifferent material into a team, with only indifferent success.

Fred later became Professor of History at Amherst. And Dan, his handsome and gifted brother, the father of the composer and Professor of Music at Harvard, Randall Thompson, subsequently became Headmaster of the Roxbury Latin School. He gave us a love of words and their meanings and introduced us to a most useful book, which I still have on my shelves: *Words and Their Ways in*

English Speech by J. B. Greenough and G. L. Kittredge. This made a great impression on me and, I daresay, on Walter, too.

It would be hard for younger readers of this chapter to picture the New York of our early childhood. They would have to erase with a giant stroke all tall buildings. Even the "Flatiron Building" hadn't broken the sky line. Upper-middle-class families lived mostly in brownstone houses with "stoops" leading up to the front door. (The so-called American basement had not yet come into being.) Here they would often sit on straw mats on warm spring evenings, while their children played tag or prisoner's base in the street. There was no danger from traffic, and the clop clop clop of the horses' hoofs would announce the coming of a hansom cab or a delivery wagon.

In such a house the Lippmanns lived, first at 121 East 79th Street, but later, when Walter was thirteen or fourteen, they moved to 46 East 80th Street, and this house remained his "permanent address" until about 1917. It was an ample dwelling, conventionally furnished with the overstuffed upholstery of the period. Its most distinctive feature was a rather impressive bay window on the first floor, made of bronze or copper.

My own family lived—until 1904—four blocks away, at No. 23 East 76th Street, the site now occupied by the National City Bank. From my bedroom window on the third floor in the back of the house, I looked down into the garden of Mr. Seth Milliken, where there was a lawn, a large flowering magnolia, and the family cow. And once, looking out of a front window, I saw for the first time a horseless carriage silently roll by. I did not know that it was electrically driven but thought that there had been a runaway and that the vehicle was following from its own momentum. Horses were much in evidence. There was a horse-drawn streetcar on Madison Avenue, and the "motorman" would stand with his feet in straw in cold weather. And on Fifth Avenue there was a stage. The coachman would hand you your change in little colored envelopes through a trap door in the ceiling. My father rode a fine chestnut mare in the park every day. And when our neighbor Mr. Clauson was ill with pneumonia, the whole of the street was covered with about six inches of tanbark to silence the noise of wagon wheels and hoofs.

Walter and I usually did not use public conveyances to go to school, but walked. We often walked home on Madison Avenue, crossing 59th Street diagonally. The Plaza Hotel was a cozy, low, red-brick structure. Mlle. Pulitzer was not on hand ready for her bath, nor was General Sherman following his good angel. At 69th Street we would pass the Presbyterian Hospital, with its bronze plaque dedicated to "the poor of New York without regard to race, creed or color." This always impressed me, as I am sure it did Walter. There was the usual "roughhousing," stealing each other's caps and swinging bundles of books on their straps, but Walter was quickly bored with such horseplay. He liked to talk. He was interested in the theater early in life. I remember his enthusiasm for *The Wizard of Oz*, and once at a Saturday matinee we saw Richard Mansfield together in *Henry V*. At home, he had a small toy stage with cutout paper figures for actors, and I have a vague recollection of a street scene with eighteen-century Georgian houses that might have represented Salem or Beacon Hill. Just what he had the characters do or say, however, has escaped me. Later he was to join his con-

CARL BINGER

temporaries in their ardent enthusiasm for Maude Adams.
Her *Little Minister, Peter Pan,* and *What Every Woman
Knows* beguiled and enthralled them. She became the pin-
up girl of the period, reaching the height of her fascina-
tion in a special performance given in Sanders Theatre at
Harvard, where members of Professor George Lyman
Kittredge's Shakespeare course were allowed to sit in the
front row.

But Walter was not all "intellectual." He was a member
of a school fraternity, which had, among other members,
Arthur Goodhart, the legal scholar, now Master of University College, Oxford. He played hockey and basketball
and went to innocent adolescent dances. He debated, and
together we defended the right of municipalities to own
and operate street railways. The next year our team won
again—this time in support of Chinese exclusion. The
coach of our debating team was a young Columbia law
student named for three presidents, Arthur Garfield Hays,
who was later to become a courageous champion of civil
rights.

Walter's first essays in journalism were on the *Junior
Record,* a slim sheet which we edited together. The editorials all began with the solemn assertion: "We, the Editors of the Record, sincerely believe." Once, we had to go
downtown in New York to visit the printer. We were still
pretty untaught in the ways of the world, and to travel by
streetcar to 23rd Street or thereabouts seemed adventure-
some. When we had finished with the printers, we had a
quarter each in our pockets. We decided to blow it in. So
we went to Childs Restaurant (well-named) and ordered
a plate of griddle cakes for twenty cents each. That left
us a nickel apiece for the ride home in the trolley. If we

had headed straight for the red-light district, we couldn't have felt more wicked. We both trembled with excitement and an awareness of wrongdoing. Such was our innocence or inexperience, and this was true in spite of the fact that we had both traveled abroad. Walter, to be sure, went to Europe every summer, and came home with a good knowledge of Italian art and other information beyond the horizons of his contemporaries. When he was quite young, he encountered Mrs. Jack Gardner in the Louvre. She took to this wonder child, and they hit up a friendship which I believe lasted for many years.

His room at home, as I recall it, had pictures of frescoes from the Sistine Chapel, and I do remember the prow of a gondola, a bust of Napoleon, and a picture of Napoleon's retreat from Moscow. For a while, Napoleon was his hero. In spite of this, he had a tender, idealistic streak in his make-up, still very evident, and he was not without sentimentality. When he was of high-school age, he wrote a piece for the *Red and Blue,* the school magazine, of which he was editor, on the child's grave next to Grant's Tomb on Riverside Drive—a study in contrasts—and another one called "The Apple Woman" about a poor lady who sold apples at the corner of 23rd Street and Fifth Avenue. These, if I am not mistaken, were among his first published writings, and they both sang songs of social significance.

The transition from school to college seemed easy for him. Both in 1904 and again in 1906, he had won the highest prize for academic achievement. He did not have to go through the agony of entrance examinations—at least, he took them without apparent agony and, of course, passed, as they said in those days, with "flying colors." When we were still sub-freshmen but had already moved

to Cambridge—it must have been just about the time of
Walter's seventeenth birthday—we spent an evening at the
Boston Museum of Fine Arts to hear a lecture by Santayana. We had gone there, of course, on Walter's initiative.
In any case, we didn't understand a word of the lecture,
and we thought it hilariously funny—especially the word
"ethos," which Santayana seemed to introduce into every
sentence, and which neither of us had encountered before.
Not many years after—perhaps two—Walter became the
friend of this bearded philosophical poet with his dark,
burning, headlight eyes, his marble brow, and his Mona
Lisa smile. In his junior year at Harvard, Walter had lunch
one day with Santayana, who said to him, "I see by my
small Spanish paper that Taft has been elected President."

Philosophy became Lippmann's "field of concentration"
—as they call it at Harvard today. But in those days of
President Charles Eliot's administration, there was the free
elective system. Anyone could choose the courses he
wished, without apparent rhyme or reason. Walter's
choices are of interest in the light of his subsequent development. He got his bachelor's degree (*cum laude*) in
three years instead of four. That meant that he took at
least one extra course each year beyond the usual requirement. Of these, seven were in philosophy, six in languages
(Latin, French, and Italian), three in English and comparative literature, three in economics (one of them with
Taussig), and one each in history and government, fine
arts, and social ethics. There wasn't a single course in
mathematics or physics, chemistry or biology. The history
professor was the famous medievalist Haskins, and the
course in government was given by that racy, well-to-do,
aristocratic Boston lawyer, A. Lawrence Lowell, who suc-

ceeded Eliot in 1909 as president of the university. The
two men were a contrast in type. Eliot was indeed the last
Puritan—supremely erect of bearing, with his shadowed
profile adding dignity and strength to his face. He spoke
with low resonance, as though he were a ventriloquist for
God; and when he presided at a meeting he would sit relaxed, but with a ramrod back, his hands in his lap, and
constantly twirling his thumbs. When he turned the reins
over to Lowell, he said that as a young man, traveling out
West, he drove through the prairies once in a buckboard
and came across a sign that said, "Choose your own rut;
you'll be in it for the next twenty-five miles." Lowell took
this advice and turned his attention and practical energy
to enlarging the university and to developing the house
plan. This changed the social life of the college.

Walter and I both lived in Weld Hall—he in number
12, I a floor above in number 20. Weld is a dreary dormi-
tory on the Yard, built in the best "anchor block" tradition. It had none of the glamour of the swell dormitories
on what was then called "the gold coast," nor the clear
Christopher Wren-like simplicity of the older buildings at
the north end of the Yard. There were few conveniences,
and though we had more privacy and space than most
college students have today, it was plain living in Weld,
without running water nearby or other modern conveniences. The atmosphere of the college was, of course,
strictly masculine. Radcliffe was still a female seminary of
bluestockinged and corseted ladies and had not yet become the coeducational, companionate grab bag for dates
that it is today. Walter's room was both more aesthetically
pleasing and more sophisticated than those of many of his
classmates. It was well stocked with books and did not

30

bristle with crossed swords, antlers, or banal banners. There was a modest array of shingles draped with ribbons and medals—the Harvard symbol of having arrived.

In the extraordinary jockeying for position and the establishment of pecking rights which take place in every Harvard class, Walter soon found his place. He was never a joiner in a big way, nor was he a remote scholar. He sat with us in many a midnight session around the liquid flames of cannel coal or before the embers of a wood fire, when conversation ranged wide. I have not wished to give the impression that I was his Boswell, or that we were constant companions, or, indeed, that I was one of the coterie of worshipers who hung on his words. There were such. I recall a Hindu student named Gupta who used to flash his white teeth at me through his beautiful brown skin and always greet me with: "Have you seen Walter?"

A few significant men (today they call them "boys") stand out—some in our class, some in classes just above or below us. Harvard was then a place of fine ferment. The literary triumvirate—Edward Sheldon, Van Wyck Brooks, and John Hall Wheelock—had just preceded us, though Sheldon was the only one of the three who had hit an early bull's-eye. Conrad Aiken followed us. And in our own class there was the poet Alan Seeger, who kept his early rendezvous with death; Heywood Broun, who later became Lippmann's fellow-columnist on the *World*; Robert Edmond Jones, then an unknown youth, who within a few years after graduation revolutionized stagecraft in America; T. S. Eliot, who tried out for the track team and wrote for the *Advocate*; and Jack Reed, the romantic reporter, who cast his lot with the Bolsheviks and died of typhus shortly after writing his famous *Ten Days That Shook the World.*

During our last year at college and for several years thereafter, many of us would go to the Chestnut Hill Farm in West Newbury, Massachusetts, on the banks of the Merrimac River about forty miles north of Boston. There, in the radiant warmth of Hazel Albertson's personality, we would meet on weekends or holidays and talk and talk and talk and bring in the hay or hoe potatoes. Hazel was then married to Ralph Albertson, a liberal Socialist with a slightly Open-Road-Walt-Whitmanish turn of mind, though a practical man. He had been an ordained minister, and by a previous marriage had had three daughters. He was president of the *Twentieth Century Magazine* and headed the executive committee that published the Boston *Common.* As such, he was Lippmann's first employer, and, later, in 1917, became his father-in-law when Walter took for his first wife Faye Albertson, a beautiful young girl who must have appealed to Walter because of her vitality rather than because they had many interests in common.

Among some of the visitors to the Farm in those days, besides Walter, were Bobby Jones and Kenneth Macgowan, Lee Simonson and Gerard Henderson, whose early death cut off what was already a brilliant legal career. There was Ernest Wescott, perhaps the most gifted of them all, who had married Hazel's sister, Florence Hammond, a charming young violinist, and Ted Behre, an intrepid liberal from New Orleans, the husband of Frances Downes, sister of the music critic Olin Downes, and there was also my engineering brother Walter, then a student at M.I.T.

At college, Lippmann wrote book reviews for the *Advocate* and was on the board of the now defunct *Harvard*

Monthly. An article that he wrote for the *Monthly* brought a knock on his door late one afternoon, and, when he opened it, there was William James—that sprightly flame of a man—who had come unannounced to see Walter and talk with him about what he had written.

James was, of course, the presiding genius of our days and lent to Harvard its characteristic ethos. His disciples— E. B. Holt, Horace Meyer Kallen, and Ralph Barton Perry —were our teachers and influenced us greatly, as did the other luminaries of the Philosophy Department—Palmer, Royce, and Santayana.

There were bright stars in English as well: Barrett Wendell, an Edwardian gentleman in spats, whose theme song in writing was "Coherence, Mass, and Unity"; that silvery-gray eminence Kittredge, whose Shakespeare course, English 2, required just the kind of accurate memory that Lippmann possessed; Neilson, later to become president of Smith, whose humor, sagacity, and integrity were enough to move any student; and Charles Townsend Copeland, affectionately known as "Copey," that eccentric spoiled darling who charmed audiences with his readings. He once made the pert remark that a party he had attended in Boston would have been a terrible bore if he hadn't been there himself, and Santayana described Boston society as resembling a faculty meeting without any business. All these men made their impression on Walter, as he did on them.

But there were extramural influences as well—a stream of distinguished visitors and lecturers, in a day when there was time enough to hear them and a seat for you when you arrived: Boutroux, the French philosopher and educator; Bergson; Florence Kelley, the Socialist and settlement worker from Hull House; James MacKaye (the brother of the poet Percy), whose *Economy of Happiness* became a sort of bible for a while; Graham Wallas, from England, who was Lippmann's friend and mentor; and Lincoln Steffens, the prince of muckrakers, who beckoned Walter down the thorny path of journalism. He came to it well prepared, for, aside from his formal education, he had read widely.

All of us swallowed the plays of Ibsen and Wilde and Shaw and the novels of Wells with eagerness. We read them with passion, as we had once read *Rab and His Friends, Bob, Son of Battle, Men of Iron,* and *Scottish Chiefs.* If William James was our hero and model, so were Shaw and Wells. Walter liked especially to read aloud some of the long Shavian speeches from *The Man of Destiny.* Perhaps this rekindled his old admiration for the Little Corporal. The Fabian movement captured our imagination, and Graham Wallas, then at the London School of Economics, was all the more valued as a visiting lecturer at Harvard for having been part of it. Wallas dedicated his book *The Great Society* to Lippmann, and since this book was published in 1914, four years after the discussion course in government that Wallas conducted and in which Walter took part, one can see what an impression this young student must have made on his teacher. But by that time (1913) Lippmann had already written his *Preface to Politics.*

The Webbs—Sidney and Beatrice—also influenced Walter by their careful, tough-minded documentation of social ills and their dedication to betterment and welfare. If Harvard was in a literary ferment, it was also, in some quarters at least, responding to the wave of social awareness that found expression in the muckraking era of Ida

Tarbell, Ray Stannard Baker, Lincoln Steffens, and Upton Sinclair, and in the trust-busting crusades of Teddy Roosevelt. Child-labor laws and minimum-wage laws were part of common concern. Walter's sensitivity and strong feeling for justice swept him along in this interest, besides the guilty conscience that sometimes goes with comfort, privilege, and a sheltered life.

He spent some of his spare time in college working among underprivileged children at Hale House, a settlement in Boston, and after the Chelsea fire, which broke out on Palm Sunday in 1908, Walter, with other student volunteers, turned his extraordinary executive talents toward helping rehabilitate the victims who had lost everything but their lives. I remember with what cool dispatch and efficiency he handled himself there—not allowing himself to be deflected from the job in hand by the devastation and misery and tragedy all around him.

Walter joined with others in founding the Social Politics Club, an organization where students and faculty met for free discussion, and he was active, as well, in the Socialist Club, of which he became president. The Socialist idea appealed to him because it seemed so rational to him, and to be rational has always been his first need. Being a rationalist, he loved to read aloud from the most irrational English poet—Algernon Charles Swinburne—and I can hear him quoting "The lilies and languors of virtue and the roses and raptures of vice" from *Dolores,* or these lines from *The Garden of Proserpine*:

> From too much love of living,
> From hope and fear set free,
> We thank with brief thanksgiving
> Whatever gods may be.

But he was never a doctrinaire Socialist, nor was he ever enthralled by the dialectics of the party as represented by Victor Berger, Morris Hillquit, and Eugene V. Debs. It is a misreading of Lippmann to think that he has swung in his more mature years from the radicalism of youth to the conservatism of age. He was never a radical. He is first and foremost a child of the Enlightenment, with a Gallic mind and a Gallic passion for reason and clarity. Given his fine mind, his diligence and discipline, and his excellent work habits, it is no wonder that his performance has been superlative. It could have been equally so in an academic career, in industry, in law, or in diplomacy. But he began his work in journalism early, and he has stuck to it consistently in spite of other invitations and attempted seductions. In his fourth year at Harvard, he combined graduate study with his first job, on a small weekly called the Boston *Common,* a periodical devoted to social reform, and a little later he joined the staff of *Everybody's Magazine.*

Then our paths separated, and for geographic reasons we saw each other less often. In June of 1917, I went to New York before embarking for overseas duty in the A.E.F. Walter and I were walking down Fifth Avenue one day on our way to the Harvard Club for lunch. As we walked along, he made one of his sage remarks: "The world we have known," he said, "is finished. It will never be the same again." How right he was. After that, to quote from *A Preface to Morals,* the "acids of modernity" bit into us.

III

Walter Lippmann, the New Republic, *and the Russian Revolution*

BY GEORGE F. KENNAN

The tale of the first years of the *New Republic* and of Walter Lippmann's part in that significant intellectual and journalistic venture could be properly told only by someone who had himself lived through this episode as a participant. Not having had this privilege, I am taking for myself a more modest task, which is to analyze, as a bit of intellectual history, the reaction of the editors of the *New Republic* to what was—along with the great war of which it was really a part—the most momentous and significant event of that time: the Russian Revolution. Then, as later, the task of digesting this phenomenon—of recognizing the deterioration of the situation of Western society which the triumph and endurance of Bolshevism in Russia implied, and of reconciling this with prevailing concepts of America's destiny as a nation—would constitute, as would no other necessity, the acid test of the validity of American liberal thought in the modern age. A review

of the response of the *New Republic* to this trial in the
years of Walter Lippmann's association with the journal
will not, of course, give the intimate picture of his life and
work at that time which someone better qualified ought
someday to give; but it may, by illuminating one of the
most significant of his professional tasks in those particular years, serve at least as a reminder of the atmosphere
of the time and of the problems that had then to be faced
by those who were endeavoring to elaborate a workable
political philosophy for the United States in the twentieth
century.

The *New Republic* had, of course, no monopoly on the
expression of American liberal thought in the years 1917-
1920. It had many other spokesmen—some of them also
people of exceptional insight and courage. Nor was there
any lack of contradiction and disagreement within the liberal camp. But there was certainly no more powerful and
lucid voice within this camp than that of the remarkable
circle of men grouped around Herbert Croly in the editorial rooms of the *New Republic*: a group that included,
in addition to Lippmann, Charles Merz, Alvin Johnson,
Philip Littell, Francis Hackett, and George Soule. In point
of sheer literary excellence alone, these men had no supe-
riors among their American contemporaries. In addition,
they were able to muster among them a catholicity of
interest, a depth of perception, a seriousness of concept, a
tolerance, and a good taste that placed their collective
effort in the foremost ranks of English-language journalism
of all time. This being the case, their view of what was
happening in Russia and of the significance of this for
American policy, was certainly as important as any other
that was being voiced on the liberal side, and may be taken

as a fair example of the manner in which many American liberals were reacting.

American opinion about Russia suffered, in the period just prior to the Revolution, from certain general distortions. It had unquestionably been deeply influenced by the many thousands of brilliantly educated and articulate Russian Jews who had emigrated to the United States in the preceding decades. These new arrivals nursed an understandable bitterness toward the Tsar's government, and their political attitudes were largely on the socialist and revolutionary side. Americans who visited Russia, moreover, found oppositionists of all colors far more eager to talk and consort with them than were the members of the Russian officialdom. The Tsar's government, in fact, made little effort to counter the negative picture of the Russian scene which was conveyed by these influences. There was, accordingly, a tendency in the West, and particularly in the United States, to be ignorant of the impressive advances, industrial, educational, and cultural, as well as in the field of civil rights, made precisely in the final years of Tsarist power, and, conversely, to exaggerate the backwardness and onerousness of the system against which Russia revolted in 1917. An inadequacy of the system to the strains of modern war (which was what primarily caused the Revolution) was often mistaken for a basic inadequacy of the system to the normal demands of the modern age.

Beyond this, the war had worked, as war always does, its own distortions of understanding. The thesis (generally incorrect, as we know today) of the treasonable pro-Germanism of the Empress, the court circles, and of the conservative, monarchist element in Russian officialdom and society—a thesis sincerely believed and assiduously propagated by liberal groups within Russia, particularly the Kadet Party—found wide credence in the Western world. But whoever was convinced that the court was both hopelessly despotic and pro-German tended to assume, conversely, that the Russian masses must be democratically minded and pro-Ally. Neither of these propositions was generally true.

Finally, as the United States swung into its own war effort, at a moment practically coincidental with the first Russian revolution, the American image of the German adversary began to suffer those distortions so characteristic for the wartime psychology of a democratic society. There was a tendency to exaggerate the malevolence of German intentions toward Russia (it was assumed, in particular, that the Germans were determined to wipe out the revolution and to reimpose a reactionary government on the country), the omniscience of German leaders about Russian conditions, and the scale of German penetration and domination of the political process in that country.

From all these deficiencies of vision, the editors of the *New Republic* suffered to some degree, along with so many others. But these minor handicaps were offset, in their case, by certain magnificent advantages of judgment. Above all, they had not yet come—by the spring of 1917— to regard the defeat of Germany as an end in itself or as the indispensable prelude to all further progress in world affairs. They were still under the sway of the detached attitude toward the war which Wilson had maintained up to America's entry into the contest. Like the President, they saw, at the time of the Russian Revolution, no possibility of avoiding America's entry; but they still viewed

the contest as one which had best not be fought to the
point of a complete military victory and subjugation of
the enemy. It would best be terminated, they felt, by a
reasonable compromise peace. Not attaching any absolute
value to the prospect of military victory, they were still
able—in contrast to many others on the Allied side—to
place the war and the Russian Revolution into perspective
with relation to each other, and to arrive in this way at
insights which must be recognized from the distance of
four decades as realistic and highly significant. Almost
alone among contemporary observers in the Allied camp,
they recognized that the revolution was itself a product of
the war and that, however happy its initial results, its
further course would be adversely affected if the war were
to be continued to the point of unconditional surrender.

... If the war is fought to a bitter end ... the ensuing revolution will be correspondingly drastic and dangerous. But if
peace supervenes before utter exhaustion sets in and without
too much victory ... it may well be revolution tempered by
law and healing.[1]

More perceptive words about the relation of the Russian
Revolution to the World War have yet to be spoken.
    On May 19, 1917, the *New Republic* recognized—as did
few others at that early moment—that failure of the Allies
to negotiate a compromise settlement and insistence on
pursuing the war to the point of unconditional surrender
would lead, inevitably, not only to a deterioration of the
revolution but also to Russia's unilateral withdrawal from
the conflict. The statesmanship of the Western Allies, it
was said, had already gone too far in its insistence "on

[1] *New Republic*, March 24, 1917.

subordinating political to military considerations." Final victory must be won by diplomacy, not by military decision alone.

Here, again, the historian can only say an admiring "amen." Only a general cessation of hostilities in 1917 could have resolved for the Provisional Government, in a manner not disastrous both to the Allied cause and to the prospects for liberal government in Russia, the problem presented by Russia's existing involvement in the World War. Only this could have prevented the triumph of the extremists and Russia's defection from the war as an act of defiance of Allied policy.

Shortly after the appearance of these perceptive warnings, Walter Lippmann left the *New Republic*, for war work in the service of the government. Following his departure—in the summer and autumn of 1917—this clear appreciation of the relationship between war and revolution began, plainly, to be obscured in the minds of the editors of the journal, under the impact of a growing emotional commitment to the Allied cause. It would be unfair to attribute this change entirely, or even primarily to Lippmann's absence, though his cool and detached temper might well have modified it. It reflected, generally, the contagion of the time. This was America's first participation in a great modern external war. The country was vulnerable, as it has never been before or since, to the massive psychosis of militancy in the democratic nation-state. As the year 1917 wore on and the first Russian revolution gave way to the second one, this psychosis began to permeate the outlook of the educated American population generally, until a point was reached where the discussion of public issues, to be intelligible and effective in the atmosphere of the day, had practically to be cast in the terms of these distortions.

The effect of all this on thinking about the Russian question was particularly unfortunate. Only a sense of detachment and relativity about the issues of the war in the West could have provided the foundation for a true understanding of what was occurring in Russia. If Germany was to be seen as the center of all evil, if the war was really to be accepted as a war to make the world safe for democracy, if Germany stood for soulless autocracy whereas we stood for the rights of common people everywhere, then, clearly, a Russia which had just thrown off the shackles of Tsarist despotism must be naturally and instinctively on our side—only reactionaries could want a separate peace.

But how to explain, then, against the background of this conviction, the dismal happenings of the final months of 1917 in Russia: the disintegration of the Russian Army, the triumph of the Bolsheviki, the move for a separate peace? This was the problem faced by the editors of the *New Republic* and by liberals everywhere. Obviously, it seemed, there must be some overriding misunderstanding. And what could this misunderstanding be? There was only one satisfactory answer. It was the confusion caused by the sordid and uninspiring "imperialistic" war aims to which the Western European Allies had committed themselves prior to America's entry into the war and to which the Russian socialists had so long objected.

In this way, the fault for the alienation of the Russian Revolution came to be seen in Western liberal circles as lying with the Allied governments of Western Europe themselves. By their refusal to take a more liberal and

43

inspiring view of the purposes for which they were fighting, a view which would appeal to the undercurrent of idealism now believed to be welling up among common people everywhere, the Allies, it was concluded, were driving out of the war a liberal Russia which at heart wanted to remain in it, and would have done so if only it could be sure that the war was being fought for worthy purposes.

This view, strongly supported by the European socialists in their agony of conscience over their own relationship to the war effort of their respective countries, found wide currency in Western liberal circles generally. It was of course the principal rationale for Wilson's Fourteen Points speech of January 8, 1918. The *New Republic*, like all the rest of the Western liberal world, received this speech with unmitigated enthusiasm. But under the sway of these misconceptions, the journal's view of the issue of limited versus total victory began to change. As the conviction gained ground that it was not by the war itself but only by the reactionary nature of the stated purposes of the Western European Allies that liberal Russia was being estranged and confounded and rendered helpless in the hands of the extremists, understanding for the necessity of a negotiated peace gradually faded. Liberal war aims came now to be seen as desirable not in the interests of the actual conclusion of an early negotiated peace, but only as a means of disrupting German morale and winning Russia back to an enthusiastic participation in the war. A decisive military victory came now to be seen, in fact, as the means by which a liberal peace, à la Wilson, was to be brought about.

In place of the realization that it was the war itself that

was dividing the West from revolutionary Russia, there came now a plea, born more of desperation and faith than of reason, for "trust" in the new Russia. By early February 1918, the editors recognized, correctly and astutely, that the Fourteen Points speech had come too late to achieve its immediate purpose; but their faith in the ultimate liberality of the Russian Revolution could not be shaken. They were persuaded that an attitude of loyalty toward the new Russia, and sympathy for her, could not fail in the end to vitiate the Bolshevik peace move and to recapture the enthusiasm of the Russian people for association—with America, at least—in the war. They were shocked and alarmed by what they took to be a hint from Lloyd George, in January 1918, that Russia, having entered into separate negotiations with the Germans, could now deservedly be left to her own devices, that it would in fact be not unjust if the Western powers were now to disregard her interests entirely in their approach to the problems of the peace. Throughout the period of the Brest-Litovsk negotiations, the columns of the *New Republic* were dominated by the fear that the West might "wash its hands of Russia."

... Russia must not be treated as a deserter, not only because her desertion is partly the fault of the Allied governments but because the Russian democracy holds the key to the peace of Europe and consequently the world. The new Russia will become the great stabilizer of the new international system or its great disturber. . . .[2]

There were, to be sure, occasional voices of clarity which questioned the assumptions underlying this view. Just at the time of the signing of the Brest-Litovsk Treaty, the

[2] *New Republic*, February 16, 1918.

New Republic carried an article by the British socialist Henry Noel Brailsford, which from the distance of four decades stands out dramatically as one of the most perceptive and prophetic of the early efforts to understand the Bolshevik political personality and its international implications. "We have still to learn one lesson about the Bolsheviki," Brailsford wrote,

and it is that they mean exactly what they say. . . . They are not pacifists, nor nationalists, nor democrats. They are working with unshakeable faith and superb audacity for one comprehensive object. It is not peace, separate or general, but social revolution. . . .

They are convinced that the social revolution must be international . . . they will have to face the hostility of capitalist civilization . . . they are thinking now of what they will have to face when the rest of us make peace.

Almost alone among observers of that day, Brailsford noted the implications of the extraordinary discipline of the Russian communist movement, in relation to its potential followers abroad. Trotsky, he wrote, had

achieved in his war what the Allies wished for in vain in theirs—unity of command. His orders run to Berlin and Vienna, to Hamburg and Budapest. There is in every country of Europe a potential element of response to these tactics.

Seeing these things, Brailsford realized that what was dividing the Russian Revolution from the West was something more than a misunderstanding, and something that would not be overcome merely by more liberal Western war aims or by expressions of faith in the Russian Revolution. "Is there a way out of the difficulty?" he asked himself; and his answer was:

46

... I doubt that there is ... they [the Bolsheviki] reason that however cautious they may be, the power of international finance will always be their implacable foe. In a sense they are right. How could they, on the basis of a completely socialized state, have resumed, after the war, the ordinary relations of trade and credit with the bankers and the trusts and the concession-hunters of the rest of the world? Sooner or later, the coalition against them would be formed.

And again:

... The belief of the true doctrinaire, that the capitalist world will always, in one way or another, scheme to destroy the first state which adopts socialism, is probably inerradicable. For my part, I think it well founded. One seems to be on the verge of one of those really inevitable disasters which make the tragedy of history. . . .[3]

Had the editors of the *New Republic* accepted the soundness of these observations and pondered deeply their implications, their disillusionment might have come somewhat sooner and less painfully than it did. The article was, to be sure, not without its effect. The journal was impelled by it to clarify its own reaction to the new power in Russia; and this it did, with characteristic courage and soundness:

The New Republic holds no brief for the present leadership of the Russian Revolution . . . . We consider the social and political programmes of the Bolsheviki wholly unsound, and wherever a general or sustained attempt is made to put them into practice the result would in our opinion be calamitous. If the Bolsheviki gained a sufficient headway in this country to become a noticeable danger, we would fight against it.[4]

[3] *New Republic*, March 9, 1918.
[4] *New Republic*, April 6, 1918.

47

But convictions contrary to Brailsford's thesis—belief in the basic liberality of revolutionary feeling in Russia; belief that the Germans as a national entity, not Western capitalism as a social force, were the natural enemies of the Russian Revolution—were now too dearly held to be immediately shattered. The conclusion of the Brest-Litovsk peace was received with incredulity. It would, the journal thought, revenge itself. Not even the German people would stand for it. They would themselves overthrow a government that tried to do anything so iniquitous to a revolutionary Russia. In any case, there was no reason for despairing of Russia or abandoning her. Between America, in particular, and the underlying spirit of the Russian people, there must be a dependable affinity.

When, therefore, in his "Red Cross speech" of May 18, 1918, President Wilson rocked the audience at the Metropolitan Opera House with his ringing declaration that "Now, as far as I am concerned, I intend to stand by Russia as well as France," he had the wholehearted and enthusiastic support of the *New Republic*.

... With President Wilson speaking for America, sooner or later the Russians must recognize her as their true friend, ready to throw all her resources into the defense of Russia against German aggression and asking for no national advantage in return. America's influence will then begin to count with the Russians on the side of moderation, order and humanity....[5]

Throughout the spring of 1918, the *New Republic*, true to this faith in the basic liberality of revolutionary Russia, stoutly opposed the growing pressures for a sanctioning of

[5] *New Republic*, May 25, 1918.

48

Japanese intervention in Siberia and for an Allied military intervention in general. Its arguments were sound and cogent. They were very much the same ones which Wilson himself was using behind the scenes to defend himself against these pressures—so much so that one is moved to suspect that he was strongly influenced by the *New Republic* in his own thinking.

During the month of June 1918, the journal underwent the same evolution of thought that seized most of official Washington and that was thought at the moment even to have prevailed with the President: acceptance of the necessity of *some* action with regard to Russia, but belief that the proper alternative to military intervention was an economic-aid program for Russia under the aegis of a high-powered civilian commission. Herbert Hoover's success in Belgium was now having an effect on American thinking. By this time, and for years to come, many Americans would be strongly attracted by the suggestion that the Bolsheviki could be confounded, and the forces of moderation in Russia revived, by a program of American aid in food and in the necessities of life. It is important to recognize that it was only by the *extension* of this aid, not by its denial, that the *New Republic* hoped for this effect. Denial of the aid was the idea that underlay the Allied blockade of later date; and this the *New Republic* opposed with all the vehemence and resolution it could muster.

As noted above, it was generally believed in Washington that it was in this direction that the President's mind was moving, and there is some evidence that up to the middle of June this was so. What caused him, unbeknownst to everyone but his Secretary of State, to change

49

his mind in the last two weeks of June and to decide, on July 4, for a purely military Japanese-American expedition to Siberia, is still a matter of conjecture. In any case, the friends and supporters of his Russian policy, among them the editors of the *New Republic*, were troubled and bewildered by the sudden change. The confused and ambiguous statement of August 3 by which, and by which alone, the President gave to the public an accounting of what he had done, did little to dispel these misgivings. The *New Republic* did not conceal its own dissatisfaction with this explanation. In mid-September, just as the American forces were arriving in Russia, it launched its first sharp attack on the intervention, thus establishing the line which it would follow consistently to the final termination of this unhappy episode. Alone, again, among Western observers, it noted with alarm that the Allied action cut all lines of communication to the Soviet government.

As the World War came to an end, the *New Republic* showed itself well aware not only of the obvious crisis which this involved for Western policy toward Russia, in the question as to what was now to be done with the Allied troops in that country, but also of the much weightier implication of the absence of any Russian government at the peace conference. It followed with sympathy, and continued support, the President's early effort at the conference to arrange for Russian participation. On February 8, 1919, in fact, as the first brief phase of the conference was coming to an end, the *New Republic* advanced its most eloquent, but also its last, defense of Wilson's Russian policy: a defense so measured and so accurate in its terms, even in historical perspective, that it well could stand today as an answer to those Soviet propagandist-historians who continue to fling at Wilson the preposterous charge of having been "the leading instigator" of the intervention.

... President Wilson is exercising as beneficial an influence on the Russian policy of the Peace Conference as he is on its general policy. He is the sincerest and most lucid friend of the Russian Revolution in the councils of the Allies. In spite of the infirmities and mistakes of his Russian policy, the Russian Revolution owes him an incalculable debt. He has prevented the French and the English governments from committing still more flagrant mistakes. He emphatically and unequivocally repudiated the policy of deserting Russia which was at one time advocated by Lloyd George. He firmly and successfully opposed the fatal plan of thrusting a large Japanese army into Siberia. He did his best to prevent the acceptance of the second plan of joint military intervention on a more moderate scale. When he finally, and in our opinion unnecessarily, yielded to the tremendous pressure brought to bear on him by the French and British governments, he yielded with certain significant reservations. . . . He acquiesced in a course of action of which he did not approve in the expectation of eventually bringing about its frustration. At the present moment he is using his influence in Paris in favor of the early and complete abandonment of military operations against the Soviet republic. . . .[6]

But the ensuing weeks brought a rapid and incisive change. The growing evidences of the failure of the conference to find any constructive answer to the Russian problem; the obvious hypocrisies and ambiguities of Allied policy toward Russia; the continued unwillingness of the Allied governments either to remove the Allied

[6] *New Republic*, February 8, 1919.

troops from Russia or to give any clear statement of the
purpose of keeping them there; the general suppression
of information about the handling of the Russian problem; Wilson's apparent helplessness in the face of Allied
policy, and his persistent failure even to state his own case
and thus to give some support to the people who had
attempted to support him: all these developments, occurring in rapid profusion, began to work a general alienation
of the liberal opinion which had heretofore followed with
such sympathy and admiration the President's efforts to
grapple with the Russian problem. Added to this was the
growing disillusionment with Wilson's performance generally at Paris, and his failure to achieve a treaty of peace
which accorded with the generous impulses of the Fourteen Points.

In March 1919, in the middle of the Peace Conference,
Walter Lippmann, who had been absent from the editorial
board of the *New Republic* for nearly two years while on
war work and on service with Colonel House's "Inquiry,"
returned to New York from Paris and rejoined the paper.
We do not know—at least the historian who works from
the published documents does not—what had been the
evolution of his thought over these intervening months.
Among the official documents we have only, as the au-
thentic product of his pen at least in its larger part, the
"Official American Commentary on the Fourteen Points,"
sometimes referred to as the "Cobb-Lippmann Memorandum," prepared in October 1918. This was a terse and
guarded public document, drafted in the hope of clarifying official policy rather than as an expression of Lippmann's own views; and one senses that his heart was not in
it. He was to observe, only shortly thereafter, that the Four-

teen Points were by that time already out of date—that in the months since Wilson had delivered his great speech of January 1918, "the world had burned its bridges," that the last terrible campaign of the spring of 1918 had destroyed the old European order to the preservation and improvement of which Wilson's words had been addressed, and had produced "the necessity of creating a new framework for international society."[7]

But we do have, as unimpeachable evidence of Lippmann's thinking on his return from Paris in 1919, the excellent treatise on the world situation, entitled "The Political Scene," which was published in the first issue of the *New Republic* (March 22, 1919) to bear his name, once more, on its masthead after his return. Here, an authoritative summary of Allied diplomacy in the final phases of the war was followed by a brilliant analysis of the faults of an Allied policy, such as that for which the French were already pressing, founded on the principles of a punitive peace against Germany and a *cordon sanitaire* against Russia. More clearly than any American of his day, Lippmann sensed the seriousness of the requirements raised for both the victors and the vanquished of the recent struggle in the West by virtue of what had occurred in Russia while they were fighting. "Lenin and Liebknecht," he wrote, "sit in the Council of Paris, and their voices are heard in every discussion. It is with them that the world is negotiating today for its own preservation." He clearly perceived the need for unity which this unseen presence brought to the peoples of western and central Europe. "The nations, with whose whole conception of

[7] Walter Lippmann, "The Political Scene," *New Republic*, March 22, 1919.

society Lenin is avowedly at war, can go forward to deal with him successfully only when they have left no formal discontent in their own rear." But this meant, he saw, that there must be a firm, hopeful, forward-looking order in Europe—an order generally acceptable to all its peoples. It would not do to return complacently, as Wilson's opponents at Paris were so ready to do, to the outworn concepts and devices of the past. In words that continue to have a warm and exciting relevance as late as 1959, he drove this lesson home:

The reason why Lenin may succeed is that the victors do not take seriously enough what he represents. They are frightened to be sure, they are even panicky, but they are not willing to subordinate every other consideration to the creation of a Europe which will be sterile to Bolshevism. They want to fight Lenin with one hand and use the other for their own purposes. They are repeating the error of those who wanted to win the war and at that same time continue to do business as usual.

Yet, perceptive and prophetic as was his grasp of the basic implications of the Russian Revolution for the affairs of the European continent, Lippmann's idea of what Bolshevism really represented suffered from certain of the misconceptions prevalent at that time in the governmental circles of the West, where people had now cut themselves off, by their own act of military intervention in Russia, from the possibility of independent observation of much of the Russian scene. Chief among these misconceptions was the failure to understand the extreme centralization of authority and the rigorous discipline that underlay the Soviet structure of power. There was still a good deal of confusion as between the rival movements of communism and anarchism. People were further thrown off by the apparent looseness of the new governmental system in Russia—by the disorderly and bewildering profusion of "soviets"—local and central. The highly disciplined, conspiratorial nature of the party itself; its role as a cohesive and ordering force behind the scenes; its relation, as a ruthless, purposeful, militant minority, to the behavior of an embittered, confused, and largely apathetic populace, lacking all sense of self-government—these things were not yet generally visible in the West. This explains how Lippmann could say that Bolshevism, being formless, had no vital center and no strategic points—that it was "a complete dissolution of centralized organization into local atoms of self-government." It explains his belief that "as far as we can see into the future Russia will be militarily impotent." It explains, finally, his own partiality to the view which was at that moment so dominant in the respective entourages of Colonel House and Herbert Hoover in Paris: the view that Russia could be drawn back into the orbit of Western thought and influence by economic assistance and trade. Seeing communism still as an anarchic populist movement, reflecting the hunger and suffering and disillusionment of the popular masses, it was easy to believe, as many people still believe today, that communism could be cured by the rising living standards and moderating influence that would come from economic intimacy with the West—that Russia, as Lippmann then put it, could be "drawn into order . . . by reestablishing the bonds of economic interdependence between her fragments and the organized society of the west"—that trade and economic assistance would spell "contact," and that with "contact" would come "that sense of the realities of government and business which is necessary to the revival of Russia."

Hoover's immediate efforts, in the weeks following Lippmann's return to the *New Republic*, to confront the new Soviet regime with an offer of American aid, which would force it either to change its spots or to suffer destruction, were abortive. The Soviet leaders, for whom politics came first, whose rule did not rest on the consent of the governed, and who now saw victory looming through the mists and horrors of the civil war, were having none of it—not, at any rate, on Hoover's terms. But it was to this faith—the faith that the political chasm between Moscow and the West could best be bridged by economic collaboration—that the editors of the *New Republic* were to cling through the remaining unhappy months of the Allied intervention and the black period of mutual bitterness and recrimination by which it was followed.

This was, inevitably, a despairing faith. It was in sharpest conflict with the fact of the intervention itself and of the progressive deterioration of the entire atmosphere underlying the relationship between Moscow and the Allied powers.

The attitude of the editors toward the Russian question in this final period of the initial encounter between Russian Communism and the West was a thoroughly troubled and unhappy one, compounded of an aversion for the ideological professions and practices of the Bolsheviki, of opposition to the intervention and blockade, of shame over the glaring weaknesses and confusions of the Allied response, generally, to the Russian Revolution and the phenomenon of communism, of a desperate belief in the basic affinity between the Russian people and the world of Western liberal thought, and of an unshaken confidence (for what else was there to build upon?) in the power of economic collaboration to heal the fateful division between old Europe and her Russian children. Even at the blackest moment, as the Russian civil war neared its conclusion and as the last of the Western troops prepared to leave Russia in frustration and confusion, the editors did not despair of the basic solubility of the problem. Pointing proudly to the now proven soundness of their own warnings about the intervention, they wrote, at the close of the year 1919:

Those who have prophesied rightly as to the tragic mistake of intervention have all along prophesied also that the restoration of peace would bring either the fall of the Bolsheviks through the rise to power of more moderate parties, or the gradual penetration of the whole soviet system with men and ideas who would modify the extremist tendencies of the present regime. This prophecy remains to be verified, but the same reasoning and the same principles which are vindicated in the matter of intervention are its basis. We believe it will be fulfilled because we believe that the Bolshevists have secured the loyalty of non-Bolshevist Russians who are defending the first revolution and the Fatherland against counter-revolutionists and invaders. We believe that peace will relax the discipline of Red Russia as it has the discipline of every other belligerent, that party interests will reassert themselves, that the opposition will compel the granting of civil liberty, and that the process of compromise will set in with the revival of industry.[8]

In the short term, these hopes were not destined to be fulfilled. The negative phase of the Russian Revolution

[8] *New Republic*, December 3, 1919, p. 10.

had as yet by no means run the terrible course that was destined to consume the hopes and energies of an entire generation of Russian people. The outlines of the more distant future were not yet visible, could not possibly be visible, to even the most prophetic eye. Only the passage of time could demonstrate what we know so well today: that the problem was really deeper than anyone in 1920 would have been able to believe—that democracy and freedom were not necessarily the natural state of mankind —that principles of government and economy abhorrent to Western thought could yet survive and flourish on great parts of the world's surface—and that a Russia still communist after the passage of decades could still come to threaten the West, but not primarily by the influence of its ideology on the industrial working masses of old Europe and America, rather by the power of its example, as a successful physical and military force, over the minds of the troubled and frustrated intellectuals of non-Europe, a non-Europe rebelling politically and psychologically, in the 1940's and '50's, as Russia herself had rebelled in 1917, against the haughty peoples of the West from whom they had imbibed both their culture and their discontents.

To the understanding and meeting of the problem presented by this new aspect of Russian Communism, Walter Lippmann was fated to make, again, in later years, an intellectual contribution second to that of no other American.

But this was not the same problem that was posed in the years 1917-1920; and the possible solutions which now suggest themselves for discussion would scarcely have been relevant to the situation of that earlier day. For the effort to understand this problem as it presented itself in those years and to suggest means for dealing with it more hopeful than any the Western governments had found, Walter Lippmann and his associates on the *New Republic* deserve the belated recognition of a normally callous and unperceptive public. Their vision had its imperfections; but these, as Gibbon said of the imperfections of Belisarius, "flowed from the contagion of the time," whereas "his virtues were his own."

No one can see into the logic of a hypothetical past which did not occur; but one is permitted to conclude that had the views of the *New Republic* on the Russian problem in the final stages and aftermath of World War I been heeded, the Western governments could have saved themselves some grievous mistakes; at least one component of the bitterness and confusion that now mark the relationship between the two worlds might never have come into existence; and the further course of Soviet-Western relations might have been perceptibly, and happily, different. What more could the editors of a weekly journal hope to have said of their labors from the distance of forty years?

IV

W. L. and the World

BY ALLAN NEVINS

When Frank I. Cobb, editor of the New York *World,* died just before Christmas in 1923, Woodrow Wilson wrote: "His death leaves a vacancy in the ranks of liberal thinkers which somebody should press forward to fill if the impulse of progress is not to be stayed." His place was already being filled by a man whom Wilson esteemed just as highly.

It took a number of components to build the bridge on which Walter Lippmann crossed from the ivory-chariot journalism of the *New Republic* (some such phrase is needed to indicate its combination of political progressivism and literary intellectualism) to the rough-and-tumble journalism of the *World.* He had become interested in the problem of informing the mass opinion of a democracy on intricate public issues, and his *Liberty and the News* in 1920 and *Public Opinion* in 1922—particularly the latter—showed the depth of his preoccupation with that puzzle. The *New Republic* under Herbert Croly had meanwhile plunged at an erratic tangent from its old path in world affairs; its break with Wilson, opposition to the

Versailles Treaty, scorn of the League, and chilly attitude toward international responsibilities marked far too barren a mood of disillusionment not to offend Lippmann's deepest convictions. He left the weekly to write his books, and the *World,* eager for his talents even before Cobb's health broke, made repeated overtures to him.

Thus it was that when the stricken Cobb came back from his last brief trip to the Maine woods in July 1923 to stay near his doctors, Lippmann was already in essential control of the editorial page. He had worked with Cobb in strengthening the staff. In the tiny office under the golden dome of the Pulitzer Building on Park Row, he dealt with events of the summer: Harding's death, relations with the Obregon Government, Prime Minister Baldwin's problems, and state affairs under Alfred E. Smith.

He was in control of an engine of information and interpretation which combined tremendous power with some sharp limitations. Editorially, the *World* had the strength and the shackles of the tradition fixed by Joseph Pulitzer, in his field a man of genius, and by Pulitzer almost alone. Cobb, in an editorial at the time of Pulitzer's death, asserted that he had been the great emancipator of the American press, meaning that he had striven to liberate it from the trammels of parties and systems and strengthen its aggressive independence.

Pulitzer had done that, and he had done much more. He had given the *World,* when he rescued it from Jay Gould in 1883, his own insatiable curiosity about every side of life, his burning interest in every force, movement, and personality of the time. He had given it his fierce earnestness on the primary issues of the hour as he saw them, so that the Pullman strike, Cleveland's Venezuela message, Bryan's stand on free silver, Cuba's revolt against Spain, T. R.'s seizure of Panama, Hughes's insurance reforms, and the Aldrich tariff were each treated as the most world-shaking question since Pope Urban led out Christendom to do battle for the Holy Sepulchre. Whoever picked up a copy of the *World* received an electric shock.

The *World* under Pulitzer, however, had much more than a fiery zest for news, great ingenuity in creating it, and a pungent, racy mode of presenting it; much more than a passionate earnestness in treating public issues. It had a set of abiding principles. To Pulitzer, the editorial page was the soul of the paper. Here was the expression of its conscience, courage, and alertness in the public interest —the justification for its existence; and while he took intermittent interest in the news pages, he gave the editorials endless care and critical attention. They had to express the principles which he had gained from his child-hood in Hungary just after the revolts of 1848, his Civil War service, his love of Goethe, his wide reading as a young man in the St. Louis Mercantile Library, his absorption in the reform movement in Missouri during Recon-struction days. He had the liberalism of the English Chartists, the German Forty-eighters, the Northern troops in the Civil War, and the postbellum independents like Carl Schurz and B. Gratz Brown, all sharpened by his Jewish idealism. Reading omnivorously, he took time to think about what he read.

And his principles were strengthened, as his expression of them was enriched, by a lively concern with written history. "Has he read Buckle?" was one of the questions he asked about Cobb when the paper considered hiring him. As an adopted citizen, he had a keener appreciation of the work of the Revolutionary Fathers, and a stronger dedication to Anglo-American ideas of civil liberty, popular government, parliamentarism, and compromise than most native-born Americans. He wanted principles constantly emphasized to give the paper consistency and staying power, "the red thread of continuous policy, which should run through it like a Wagnerian motif."

Such a journal, pulsing with interest, made warm admirers and bitter enemies. The admirers tended to overlook its limitations, which were partly the defects of its virtues. Pulitzer's passionate conviction made it overemphatic and disinclined to take account of the niceties of fact and idea in which exact truth lies. Seeing everything in black and white, the paper stated its denunciation of the sable side and espousal of light in strident tones. It was by no means free from partisanship, though Pulitzer liked to pretend that it was. Like other newspapers which clung to the liberalism of the Forty-eighters and of Cobden, Mill, Bagehot, and other giants of the Manchester school, it found the Democratic halls more comfortable than the Republican. "J. P." admitted to Cobb in 1910 that his secretary had been right when he remarked, "You seem to want to make another Democratic President." In fact, the *World*, more than any other journal, could be termed the precentor of the Democratic press, for in campaign after campaign it led the other Democratic sheets to the charge. Of course, it did not hesitate to break with the party on occasion, as in its repudiation of Bryan in 1896; it was never uncritical, as its attacks on Cleveland's mode of marketing his bond issues and its characterization of Wilson's appeal for a Democratic Congress in 1918 as an "inexcusable error" showed. But in general it was true to the party.

This partisanship subtly limited its independence. Much more serious was the fact that liberalism of the John Stuart Mill–Gladstone–Grover Cleveland type, not without a strong dash of William Graham Sumner's doctrines, became outworn in the new century and inhibited the *World* on issues where it should have shown radicalism. It liked to reprint Cleveland's message vetoing a grant of free seed to drought-stricken Texas farmers on the ground that, as Cleveland put it, the people should always support the government, but the government should never support the people. This was sound doctrine for an older era, but not for the new day.

Frank I. Cobb had deepened rather than broadened the Pulitzer tradition. He also saw the contemporaneous scene in blacks and whites; he also liked the strident tone. The *World*'s motto, as given it by Pulitzer on his sixtieth birthday—"an institution which should always fight for progress and reform; never tolerate injustice or corruption," and so on—was full of the most positive expressions. In one sentence of half a dozen lines it dealt with "public plunder," "predatory plutocracy," "predatory poverty," and "demagogues," with three uses of the words "fight" or "attack," three of "always," and four of "never." That sentence was not so much a trumpet call as the roar of a Big Bertha. Such were the terms which studded Cobb's able, hard-hitting editorial page.

In the chaotic scene before, during, and just after World War I, this Kansas-born, Michigan-reared journalist had ample scope for the sledge-hammer style he had forged on the Detroit *Free Press*. As editor, Cobb had not a neutral drop in his ink bottle. As flamingly as the Archangel Michael fought Lucifer, he fought the Red Scare and the Sedition Act; the Ku Klux Klan with all its Kleagles; Wayne B. Wheeler's tyrannical apparatus for enforcing the Prohibition Amendment; J. P. Morgan's "financial oligarchy" and the New Haven Railroad's "financial tyranny"; the misdeeds of capital in the great steel strike just after the war, and the outrages of the McNamaras in the California labor troubles. He never feared overstatement. "The death-blow to Jeffersonian democracy"—this was the Eighteenth Amendment. "Nonsense" which "touches the depths of imbecility"—this was preparedness propaganda. "A gift for intrigue unequalled since Aaron Burr"—this was T.R. His epigrams were merciless. "Mr. Hanna knew how to turn money into government. Mr. Morgan knew how to turn government into money." Personally Cobb was all gentleness and kindliness, and such statements simply measured the fervor of his devotion to civic decency.

Lippmann had no sooner taken the helm in 1923, to hold it until February 27, 1931, than it was plain that the *World* had an editor of very special gifts. The obituary editorial on his predecessor, which he probably wrote, remarked: "As editor of THE WORLD, Mr. Cobb taught scorn of narrowness in American intellectual and political life." This was true, but the page became much broader under Lippmann, more flexible, and more entertaining. It changed also in other respects.

The greater breadth arose partly because of Lippmann's own versatility, and partly because new talents were enlisted. Maxwell Anderson, who had served under Cobb, departed to devote himself to drama. But Charles Merz, later editor of the New York *Times*, came to bear an exceedingly able and dependable hand in treating many subjects. James M. Cain, later to gain fame as a novelist, discussed a large body of social topics with an unusual combination of humor, grace, and penetration. W. O. Scroggs, in time Dean of Graduate Studies at Louisiana State University, treated economic questions. John L. Heaton, a veteran lieutenant of Pulitzer, continued to deal expertly with municipal and state affairs. The author of this contribution was expected to supply historical perspective as well as experience gained on the *Nation* and the *Evening Post*. One aspect of Lippmann's competence as editor was the inspiration he gave these men, the skill he showed in revising and bettering their copy, and the affectionate devotion he won from all of them. It was his own writing, however, that gave high distinction to the newspaper.

He was as much a liberal, an anti-Machiavellian, as Pulitzer had been, and was as much an earnest, painstaking craftsman as Cobb. But he was also what neither of them had been, a great humanist. No more inclined than they to mute his convictions or hide his seriousness under a mask of irony, he uttered his views with the direct urgency that had always marked the editorial page. But he was more conscious than other newspapermen of the fact that only reasoned argument, in the last analysis, can overthrow ignorance and prejudice, and that reason at its best means logic and subtlety, not just sledgehammer assertion. The black-and-white view of affairs, as in a Thomas Nast cartoon, disappeared from the *World* page in favor of something more closely representing a Winslow Homer painting, with a strong central effect set off by delicate shadings and background chiaroscuro. Like Lincoln, he knew how to use great logical clarity in treating an issue without oversimplifying that issue. And his writing gave evidence that at different times he had been interested in art, sociology, government, anthropology, and economics, and that he had read discursively.

These were the two main facets of his humanism: reliance on reason and an informed interest in a wide range of subjects. They enabled him to add a new dimension to the *World*, which, contrary to a general expectation, was not at all a *New Republic* dimension. It could not be. The weekly journal is above the melee, a critical spectator; the daily journalist is down in the dust of the arena, a participant in its struggle.

The transition to this new type of editorial work was for two reasons a severe test of character. To begin with, it tested his practicality. It measured the real utility of his sympathy with the politician trying to improve city and state affairs a bit; the worker striving to get a fairer deal for his family; the farmer struggling to climb out of the ditch where the postwar slump had flung him; the teacher, minister, and social worker hurt less because he was underpaid than because he was under-respected. The issues were harshly real, they came up every hour, and they had to be dealt with not in cool essays but in terms that would appeal to the ward committeeman and the union organizer. The *World* fortunately got an editor schooled rather by Graham Wallas, Mayor George Lunn, Newton D. Baker, and Woodrow Wilson than by Herbert Croly; a humanist with a vision of a more mature society, and a humanitarian whose sympathies were tempered by a sense of what could and could not be done.

It was a severe test also because he had to deal reason-

ably with issues in what was probably the most unreasonable, irresponsible, and repulsive decade of American
history. It was the decade of Ma Ferguson, Al Capone, the
emergent Huey Long, Aimee Semple McPherson, and
Charles E. Coughlin, the radio priest. It was the decade of
Big Bill Thompson in Chicago, Jimmy Walker in New
York, and the little Green House on K Street in Washington. Cross-channel swimming, flagstaff-sitting, and dance
marathons divided public attention with the promotional
activities of Tex Rickard in pugilism. Calvin Coolidge
kept unworried, as he explained, "by avoiding the big
problems," and the United States in all its power cowered
from the World Court like an elephant from a mouse.
Successive administrations were hostile to labor, indifferent to the farmers, generous to businessmen seeking tariff
favors, and wedded to tax programs that let wealth filter
down from the top. Repeated race riots took place, and
religious intolerance seldom reared an uglier head than
in the presidential campaign of 1928. All this made a
pattern especially repugnant to a journal of the *World*'s
traditions.

Yet Lippmann, as a believer in reason, aware of the
emptiness of mere invective, gave readers not merely the
keenest interpretive comment on events, but also the most
tolerant of intelligent appraisals. Doubtless it was keen
largely because it was tolerant. Of course, he and everyone
else knew that the decade contained many achievements
that were wholesome, unselfish, and durably constructive.
The 1920's produced more good fiction, poetry, and drama
than any ten-year period since the 1850's. Standards of
education, health, comfort, and culture—particularly in
appreciation of art and music—were rising. His tolerance,

68

however, was rooted in a comprehension of society and its innumerable problems, not in satisfaction over current gains. If any feeling was ingrained in him, it was hatred of intolerance. He wished to make readers understand themselves, take a reasoned view of difficulties and disorders, and give up prejudices and antagonisms. This attitude he explicitly stated in 1925 in his *The Phantom Public*:

We have had . . . Nebraska, which discovered that if you wish to prohibit liquor in Nebraska you must prohibit it everywhere. Nebraska cannot live by itself alone, being too weak to control an international traffic. We have had the socialist who was convinced that socialism can maintain itself only on a socialist planet. We have had Secretary Hughes who was convinced that capitalism can exist only on a capitalist planet. We have had all the imperialists who could not live unless they advanced the backward races. And we have had the Ku Klux Klansmen who were persuaded that if you organized and sold hate on a country-wide scale there would be lots more hate than there was before. We have had the Germans before 1914 who were told that they had to choose between "world power or downfall," and the French who for some years after 1919 could not be "secure" in Europe unless everybody else was insecure. We have had all conceivable manifestation of the impulse to seek stability in an incalculable environment by standardizing for one's own apparent convenience all those who form the context of one's activity.

Lippmann's attachment to reason, stated carefully and logically, of course irritated some unreasonable men. His insistence that both his condemnations and commendations be qualified wherever justice demanded a discriminating statement irritated many partisans. People who liked the Irish recipe of a word and a blow—the blow first—demanded: "Hang it, why can't he make up his mind which side he is on, and tell us bluntly?" In several essays of the period, he emphasized his belief that whereas in our early history some of our primary national problems could be called simple, now not one had that quality; they had all become "subtler and greater." It was precisely this emphasis on complexity and subtlety, combined with his anxiety to walk all around an issue in search of truth, which downright people, hoping to see their prejudices reinforced in downright language, deprecated. But Lippmann, like Lincoln, distrusted passion and emotion. He disliked tub-thumping for one-sided causes. "Look here," a colleague once heard him say, "I can't always be raising a flag and rushing off to battle." Or, as he put it in his speech to the Academy of Political Science just after the discontinuance of the *World*:

It is vain to suppose that our problems can be dealt with by rallying the people to some crusade that can be expressed in a symbol, a phrase, a set of principles or a program. If that is what progressives are looking for today they will look in vain. For the objectives to which a nation like this could be aroused in something like unanimity are limited to a war or to some kind of futile or destructive fanaticism. Our objectives in time of external peace and of internal sanity are beyond the power of any man or faction or party to formulate or declare. They are too many-sided. They have to be discovered by the solitary effort of too many minds. They have to be elucidated by continual free discussion. They have to be accepted with at least a modicum of good will. They have to be proved by experiment rather than imposed by authority. They cannot be deduced from a formula and imposed by legislative fiat.

These are the ways of liberty. They are laborious and often

disappointing. But however we may momentarily forget them and seek some shorter road to righteousness, or prosperity, or justice, we are driven back to them sooner or later. . . .

These were the basic ideas and methods of Lippmann as editor; what of their specific applications? His associates often disagreed with him and sometimes argued with him. This was sometimes because they thought him too subtle, too inclined to take the many-sided view, but more often because he did not have the instinctive "feel" for American politics that Cobb or Rollo Ogden or William Allen White had. But certainly the staff never failed to greet the new day with a pleased anticipation of the incisiveness and originality of the views he would express. The editors met with him, sometimes singly, more often in a group, in his little office around eleven. Rollin Kirby was usually there with several alternative sketches for the day's cartoon; W. L. would approve one and dismiss him with a jest on the ease with which he earned his salary. Sometimes he would then tell us his ideas for the day's leader; sometimes it was already in the linotypist's hands, for he had a way of writing it at home in his minute script, so heavily corrected that compositors swore over it.

Except during a political campaign, international affairs occupied him more than any other subject—the League, the World Court, disarmament, troubles in Mexico, Haiti, and Central America, war debts, foreign loans, and the Dawes and Young plans. The ignorance and indifference displayed by Harding and Coolidge in this field, the timidity of Secretary Hughes before blustering isolationist senators, and the clumsiness of Secretary Kellogg, gave ample scope for prodding. Next to these subjects, Lippmann and his staff were chiefly concerned with the innumerable invasions of basic human liberties in the years 1923-31: the Ku Klux Klan, Prohibition enforcement, offenses against labor, ebullitions of racial and religious intolerance, and the excesses of 200-per-cent Americans in policing any group they chose to label Red. No day lacked its opportunity for sad or indignant comment.

Third in importance came the broad field of state and national politics. Here the traditional Democratic coloration of the *World* was deepened by the personal admiration which W. L. and other *World* men had for Al Smith, their distaste for the subservience of the Harding and Coolidge administrations to big business, and their special scorn for the frigid impotence of Coolidge in facing—or, rather, refusing to face—national problems. The scorn extended to others. In a valedictory editorial on the Coolidge era, "Nothing Ventured, Nothing Lost" (March 4, 1929), Lippmann remarked: "Surely no one will write of these years since August, 1923, that an aggressive President altered the destiny of the Republic. Yet it is an important fact that no one will write of these same years that the Republic wished its destiny to be altered." Another acrid comment on the Harding-Coolidge spirit was well summed up in its title: "So Corrupt, So Partial, So Feeble" (August 12, 1924). At all times Lippmann insisted that modern democracy needs strongly asserted leadership. Finally, while he was never indifferent to such matters as education, housing, and health, he rested his spotlight again and again on the need for an enlightened policy on immigration.

Some of these subjects cannot be reviewed without rehearsing the history of the time. But on others a few words of explanation may be interesting as well as enlightening.

In foreign affairs, the *World* was deeply angered by the cowardice of the Coolidge administration in letting a knot of arrogant isolationists balk American entrance into the World Court. This added an insulting gesture to the destructive scuttle-and-run policy of the government on the League. When the President, confronted with a choice between the Court and maintenance of a few picayunish reservations by senatorial desk-pounders, came down in a Kansas City speech against the Court, Lippmann published an editorial with the sarcastic heading "Coolidge the Lion-Hearted," which historians should always consult as an exposure of the President's littleness. The *World* never believed that isolationism was anything but a sham. Lippmann wrote of it as "Isolation, Ltd.," which did not achieve disengagement but did produce many dangers. While neither he nor the staff had any faith in the Kellogg-Briand Pact, they did see it as a crablike retreat toward a partial assumption of world responsibilities, and Lippmann wrote in "The Signing of the Treaty" (August 28, 1928): "The fact that Mr. Kellogg went to Paris is historically more important than anything he did there." To the *World*, the perils engendered by America's abdication of its proper responsibilities in the global situation were very real, and as the years passed became more formidable. In an editorial, "The Danger in Europe" (December 1, 1927), Lippmann struck a chord soon to seem prophetic:

There are . . . vast and powerful interests in Europe committed not to peace but to a revision of the peace which now

73

exists. . . . The diplomatic situation is so ingenious that it is dangerous. . . . There is no need to be an alarmist to see that Europe is drifting rather rapidly toward a situation very much like that which existed in 1914.

The greatest single achievement of the *World* in foreign affairs, however, concerned Mexico. Coolidge and Kellogg in 1925-26, with plenty of help from President Plutarco E. Calles and a stiff-necked ambassador, let the United States and Mexico drift into a dangerous embroilment. Religious bitterness added to the difficulties. American intervention seemed alarmingly imminent. In a signally well informed and forcibly written series of articles, the *World* analyzed the situation, exposed the selfish interests behind the clamor for intervention, and awakened the public to the drift of affairs. More than any other single agency, it compelled the adoption of a wiser policy; and Lippmann felt special gratification when in 1927 his friend Dwight W. Morrow was sent down to straighten out the situation.

In contending for a fairer attitude toward Mexico, the *World* found its chief opponent not in Coolidge or Kellogg, but in public clamor, much of it artificially promoted. To be sure, Lippmann criticized State Department aggressiveness severely. One editorial, "Stop This Bullying," asked for decent courtesy: "It is about time that we stopped raising our voices and banging the table every time the Mexican Government displeases." But propaganda for intervention was the main target. The *World* was courageous in insisting that although the treatment of the church seemed rough, "it should be recalled how rapacious, up to the time of Juarez's reformation, was the appetite of the religious orders for choice land; how constant was ecclesiastical interference in politics even under Diaz, and how determinedly church influence once opposed advances in most directions." The treatment of great landowners seemed rough; but "it must be remembered that the landless peon was recently the typical Mexican figure." Once, Secretary Kellogg visited the *World* office. The paper had proposed that since neither Chile nor Peru would give up Tacna-Arica, these largely desert provinces be ceded to Bolivia as a much-needed sea front; and Kellogg came to ask that the *World* reiterate this proposal, and continue reiterating it.

In domestic affairs, Lippmann so mercilessly raked the do-nothingism of Coolidge that it is a wonder the President ever asked him to lunch—as once he did. "Time to Burn" ran a typical caption over an editorial on the neglect of a sick industry, coal. "Coolidge's policy toward Congress is to let live and let slide," Lippmann remarked. The President hated to take stands, he disliked trouble and worry, he was afraid of rows, "and he is gun-shy after the repeated drubbings administered to him by his party in Washington." One of the crusades into which Lippmann threw himself with gusto was that against the Mellon monopoly in aluminum, a salvo of editorials accompanying a series of savage news articles at the beginning of 1926.

Timid and greedy attitudes in foreign affairs—the effort to collect foreign debts over high tariff barriers, for example—were of a piece with the dodging of problems and grant of special favors in the domestic field. Indeed, they were of a piece with the general temper of the times. "This generation," wrote Lippmann in the mid-twenties, apropos of one heroic maritime exploit, "has not had

much cause to rejoice at the dignity of man. It has seen
even the heroism and sacrifice of the war turned to mean
ends and lost in confusion and muddle. It has seen a
stupendous prosperity run into soft and cautious living."
A sense of revolt against the fat, self-complacent arrogance
of many of those in political and economic power at the
time gave edge to the blade the *World* wielded in its
before-noted defense of basic human liberties. These liberties were always being assailed on some front, by some
would-be tyrant; and the *World* used both argument and
satire to defeat the invaders.

Now it was Speaker Nicholas Longworth proposing to
exile every man who preached Bolshevist doctrines; the
World suggested the knout and a chain of Montana salt
mines instead. Now it was the Labor Department, holding
for deportation at Ellis Island a countess who had committed adultery in South Africa, where it was no crime;
Lippmann first used as editorial the passage in the New
Testament giving the story of Jesus and the woman taken
in adultery, heading it "The Other Way," and then dug
up the statistic that, over a recent period, 300,000 Americans had been granted divorces, and at least 100,000 of
the cases involved adultery. Now it was federal enforcement officers, under the Volstead Act, passing over notori-
ous gangster hangouts to padlock the Hotel Brevoort, one
of the most civilized spots in New York. Now it was some
new attack on the rights of labor. No American journal was
so much feared and hated by those who abused civil liberties as was the *World* under Lippmann. It won many a
skirmish, and, even in the long running battle against
Prohibition, it made progress. On December 17, 1925, in a
leader headed "The Prohibition Tide Has Turned,"

Lippmann declared that at last the editors were certain that modification was coming; and in a few years this faith turned to certainty of outright repeal.

That Herbert Hoover was a much stronger President than his predecessors, the *World* never doubted, but his failure properly to exert his strength seemed to Lippmann unforgivable. When the Smoot-Hawley tariff simultaneously offered new gifts to special plutocratic interests and struck a staggering blow at international stability, Lippmann powerfully expressed his sense of outrage. In vain had a thousand American economists protested against the bill; in vain had one foreign government after another registered its protest. When Hoover signed the measure, W. L. brought down to the office an editorial with the heading "Why?"—which he changed to "Can Anyone Explain?" (June 18, 1930). Why had Hoover not used his vast power and personal authority to guide his party in shaping a tariff suited to America's economic constitution and its new position in the world? Why had he sat inert for well over a year?

The tariff-making was a slow affair taking fifteen months; there were a thousand chances to take firm hold of it; there were endless precedents for taking hold of it.

In fact, Mr. Hoover was implored by the leaders of his own party to take hold. He was publicly challenged again and again to take hold. . . . He would not take hold. He saw his party break up in the Senate. He would not take hold. He saw a bill being framed which practically nobody except the authors really approved. He would not take the lead. He saw his party get out of hand. He saw his own popularity deflated at a terrifying rate. For some reason, which is beyond the scope of ordinary explaining, he surrendered everything for nothing.

77

He gave up the leadership of his party. He let his personal authority be flouted. He accepted a wretched and mischievous product of stupidity and greed.

Why? To what end, for what result, has he made this dreadfully humiliating sacrifice?

In many of the *World*'s battles, the editorial page and the news pages acted in close co-operation; in others they did not. Lippmann's authority, even after he was formally designated editor of the *World* in February 1929, was limited to "the Page." In an older era, great metropolitan editors deployed all the forces of their newspapers as a corps commander deployed his infantry, cavalry, and artillery in combat. Greeley, the consummate example, had seen to it that in the contest against slavery, or the movement for the homestead bill, not only the editorials, but the Washington correspondence, the metropolitan news, the financial column, the carefully selected letters, and even the theatrical and book criticism, all maneuvered as one. That day had passed. On the highly compartmentalized *World*, Herbert Bayard Swope controlled the news columns, as other men, like the talkative Don C. Seitz, until his retirement, controlled the business office. While Swope and Lippmann worked in perfect amity, they had little in common either inside or outside journalism; and Lippmann's concern with the news was limited to occasional pleas for coverage of special subjects, suggestions of news sources, and an effort to see that gifted young men like Laurence Stallings and William Bolitho were given the opportunities they coveted.

Still, on Prohibition, on the struggle against the Klan (largely ended, so far as its crusading phase went, when Lippmann arrived, but continuously important down through 1928), in the successive political campaigns, and on various discrete issues, W. L. did his best to see that news policy and editorial policy were co-ordinated. I daresay that to him the excellent Washington correspondence written by Louis Seibold, the expert musical criticism and comment written by Samuel Chotzinoff, and the remarkably good labor news by John J. Leary, Jr., meant rather more than the "prima donna page" on which Alexander Woollcott, Franklin P. Adams, and Heywood Broun starred —friendly as he was with these men. He appreciated and commended good writing wherever it could be found in the paper. Giving meticulous attention to his own style, he detested slipshod English and cherished any colleague who, like James M. Cain, rewrote and sandpapered his contributions until they seemed perfect. Once he caught Cain up on an error with the remark, "You, of all men!"; and he once rebuked me for using "farther" when I should have written "further." A particularly vivid or able piece of reporting was sure of his praise.

Sometimes, of course, his own editorial on an event had more news value than the peg, or illumined the inner meaning of the event in a memorable way. An illustration of this fact which is at the same time an example of his warm humanity is his editorial essay of 1924 on Cecilia Cooney. This girl for several months had floated before New York's vision as the "bobbed hair bandit," an attractive Robinetta Hood who held up pedestrians and flitted off on alluring new adventures. Then she was jailed, and a probation officer reported her real story. Cecilia in her twenty years had been touched by most of the city's agencies of righteousness: the Children's Aid Society, the Department of Charities, the church. At fifteen, she had worked in a brush factory, and at sixteen as a laundress; she married and became a mother; she turned to crime. The record was not in the least romantic. "For there in the place of the dashing bandit was a pitiable girl; instead of an amusing tale, a dark and mean tragedy; instead of a lovely adventure, a terrible accusation." W. L. went on:

This is what twentieth century civilization in New York achieved in the case of Cecilia Cooney. Fully warned by the behavior of her parents before her birth, the law allowed her parents to reproduce their kind. Fully warned when she was still an infant, society allowed her to drift out of its hands into a life of dirt, neglect, dark basements, begging, stealing, ignorance, poor little tawdry excitements and twisted romance. The courts had their chance and they missed it. Charity had its chance and missed it. The church had its chance and missed it. The absent-minded routine of all that is well-meaning and respectable did not deflect by an inch her inexorable progress from the basement where she was born to the jail where she will expiate her crimes and ours.

For her crimes are on our heads too. No record could be clearer or more eloquent. None could leave less room for doubt that Cecilia Cooney is a product of this city, of its neglect and its carelessness, of its indifference and its undercurrents of misery. We recommend her story to the pulpits of New York, to the schoolmen of New York, to the lawmakers of New York, to the social workers of New York, to those who are tempted to boast of its wealth, its magnificence, and its power.

Like all other papers and editors, the *World* and Walter Lippmann could be accused of shortcomings and errors. In the long view, it is certainly not important that sometimes W. L. perhaps supported the wrong candidate, espousing Robert Wagner for the Senate when he should have chosen the courageous James L. Wadsworth; that he perhaps displayed an exaggerated earnestness in dealing with the Dayton trial on evolution; that he was perhaps too intellectually cool when he came to the Sacco-Vanzetti case, and showed too much judicial aloofness until Felix Frankfurter awakened him with a transcript of the hearing. Some criticisms have been unfair. Heywood Broun, who left at the time of the Sacco-Vanzetti executions, was not estopped from free comment on the main matter; he was estopped from violent attack on the men who could still save Sacco and Vanzetti, Governor Fuller and his advisers. (Broun and Lippmann were temperamentally antipathetic; Broun once remarked that W. L. could score a field goal for Harvard and a touchdown for Yale on the same play, a statement that doubtless amused Walter as much as anybody.)

Lippmann's oft-quoted remark on Franklin D. Roosevelt's lack of demonstrated qualifications for the presidency, however unfortunate—and it was unfortunate—was not unfair at the time it was made, January 8, 1932. But this is a trifle compared with the immense service the *World* did in its continuously effective support of Al Smith as governor, and in its long battle to give him the national prominence and influence that were his due. In 1929, the *World* was one of the potent agents in persuading Franklin D. Roosevelt to accept the nomination for governor. Lippmann and his staff never during the boom of the twenties foresaw the stock-market crash and depression; but who did foresee them? Various men have made lists of Lippmann's inconsistencies. While consistency may not be Emerson's hobgoblin of little minds, it is certainly neither attainable nor desirable for an editor following the rush of the day's news; and on matters of basic principle, the *World* steered an unchanging course.

Throughout Lippmann's editorship, but particularly after 1928, the *World* as a business entity was inexorably slipping downhill. The competition of the *Times* and the *Herald Tribune* on one side and the tabloids on the other weakened it so that it did not survive the sharp initial squall of the economic storm. Had the news policy emphasized comprehensiveness instead of selectivity, had the business management been more sagacious, and, above all, had Ralph and Herbert Pulitzer, after their father's death, resolutely poured into the paper more of the profits it long made, the story would have been different. The *World* might have survived the squall, and during the years of the New Deal and World War II have remained an invaluable citadel of American democracy. It is a simple statement of fact that on the day it went down, with Lippmann's felicitous quotation from John Bunyan closing its last editorial, millions of people felt a sense of personal bereavement, and not a few shed tears.

Significantly, among many of these people grief over the loss of one of the few truly great newspapers in American history was accompanied by an instant anxiety over the question, "What will this event mean to the editor? What will he now do?" We hoped, but we could not be sure, that the years on the *World* would prove simply an apprenticeship for more valuable labors in a larger sphere. The next years were dark enough for the country and the globe, but one bright fact was the realization of this hope.

V

The Early Personal Journalists

BY ARTHUR KROCK

"Personal journalism" has, with all solemnity, been buried many times. The last occasion of this funeral service over its supposed corpse was in 1921 at the death of Henry Watterson of the Louisville *Courier-Journal*.

But though personal journalism has often been buried, it has never been obliging enough to die. In proof of this, the general and particular subject of this book relates to personal journalism as it is practiced today when editorial commentators sign their names and their comment is published in hundreds of paper through syndication.

Syndicated publishing is comparatively new, having begun in this century. Another new aspect is that publishers have surrendered to the syndicated editorial commentator the opinions on matters, momentous and trivial, that formerly they hired editors to express locally. New also in personal journalism is that this material is published in newspapers of other countries, and in other languages.

But these are the only new factors in an institution of journalism, both free and captive, so venerable that it has

83

existed since the manufacture of paper and ink and the invention of the printing press. Moreover, even the talented exponent of the trade who is the subject of this book has not, I think, yet exceeded the fame of certain of his predecessors at home or abroad.

Editorial commentators may exercise more influence now than then. This is an imponderable beyond my power to resolve, and I doubt that anyone can reduce it to a mathematical formula. But in the flush times of the personal journalists, their editorials, signed or unsigned, though they appeared only in their own newspapers, were lifted as news dispatches by the press associations and by individual news correspondents. This was regular practice, for example, when Watterson dug his mighty pen into a national or international situation.

As I have noted, the editorial commentator has a long ancestry in journalism. But this exegesis may conveniently begin with the Liberal Democratic convention of 1872 at Cincinnati, at which Horace Greeley was nominated for President.

Gathered there, as frankly engaged on the spot in influencing the choice of nominees as Walter Lippmann, for instance, through the impersonal medium of the printed page, is in daily proposing American foreign and domestic policy for the President and Congress, were the newspapermen who called themselves the "Quadrilateral." These four were Watterson; Murat Halstead, editor of the Cincinnati *Commercial*; Samuel Bowles, editor of the Springfield (Massachusetts) *Republican*; and Horace White, editor of the Chicago *Tribune*. The subjoined extracts demonstrate how near to the present were their formula and their undertaking.

This is a major difference between the operations of the Quadrilateral at Cincinnati in 1872 and their modern descendants. The four editors not only set out to be king-makers, but they asserted it, and operated openly. However, we already have the testimony of the elder of the Alsop brothers on private activities to produce acts of government—for example, Franklin D. Roosevelt's 1940 trade with Great Britain of British bases for United States overage destroyers. And in publicly recording this, Joseph Alsop merely has been franker than several of his colleagues in the editorial-comment trade.

The press cabal failed at Cincinnati when Greeley got the nomination at a convention where, except for the Bull Moose gathering in 1912 and Henry A. Wallace's Progressive party assemblage in 1948, there was the weirdest cometogether in American political history of cranks, crackpots, and practical politicians.

One reason for the failure of the Quadrilateral was that it innocently admitted to the inner councils Greeley's right-hand man at the New York *Tribune*, its managing editor, Whitelaw Reid. The objection made to his admission—by Halstead and Bowles—was that, unlike these editors in chief, he was a "subordinate." But, this overruled by the others, Reid wrought well for his presidential-candidate boss. And, looking back on the incidents forty-five years later, Watterson wrote this in his memoirs, *Marse Henry*: "The Quadrilateral was nowhere. It was done for. The impossible had come to pass. The Quadrilateral was knocked into a cocked hat—reformers hoist by their own petard!"

As a sort of advance publicity agent for the Quadrilateral, Watterson, in the *Courier-Journal*, March 29, 1872, asserted:

Not in this country are four men of more pluck, muscle and power than Horace Greeley, Samuel Bowles, Murat Halstead and Horace White. The four great newspapers which they control could, by acting in concert, turn the scales of the coming contest. But, unsupported by them, the Cincinnati Convention may as well slide into the lap of the International Democracy for, unsupported by them, it will prove merely a faction of the Republican Party, and be lost in the Democratic organization which will follow it. . . .

The Quadrilateral, though it did in large degree "act in concert," notably did not "turn the scales."

But Watterson's instincts as a news reporter getting the better of him as a political manager, he added,

The convention, we think made a grave mistake when the business came to the nomination of a ticket. We have profound respect for the sincerity and honesty of Horace Greeley's character and our sympathies far more readily go out to him than to Charles Francis Adams, who, although patriotic and reliable, is unquestionably as cold and impassible as a block of granite hewn from one of his native New England hills. Most Democrats, however, have come to the conclusion that Adams was the man for the Liberals to put forward, and therefore when the indications were on Thursday that he would receive the nomination, Democrats, very generally manifested gratification. Nothing is more certain that Adams' nomination would have secured the Democratic support. As the case stands, a Democratic convention must of necessity be held for consultation—a convention in which the party shall take counsel regarding the proper course to be pursued. Under any circumstances, the calling of a National Convention would have been desirable, and now it is more essential than ever. . . .

86

The Democrats took this advice and held the convention. But they adopted Greeley as their candidate also, and President Grant was overwhelmingly re-elected.

Each member of the Quadrilateral had inaugurated the modern system of syndication by printing in his own paper the product of the other three, plus his own. Proceeding in this pioneering, they all, on May 4, 1872, published a vigorous protest by Bowles of a New York dispatch to the *Commercial* saying that Greeley was told by Senator Reuben E. Fenton of New York that Bowles had been circulating "prejudicial lies" against the candidate. Bowles wrote:

Mr. Greeley's unexpected nomination, seems to have turned his usual level head; he certainly strikes quite wild here. That Fenton came to Cincinnati in the Davis intrigue [Judge David Davis of Illinois] is too plain to those who know the history of this week's contest . . . to admit of a doubt; that he fled back to Washington when he found it was discovered and broke it up, and that he must confront the question of earnestly supporting Mr. Greeley's nomination or selling him out, lies upon the surface of that week's history.

Mr. Greeley owes very little of his success to Governor Fenton. He owes it, first, to those who boldly threw themselves into the arena and smashed the Davis job that had been so industriously put up in Washington and in New York and Pennsylvania and Illinois and deep in which were some of those who were professing to be Mr. Greeley's earnest friends and advocates; and, second, he owes it to the appearance of Frank Blair and Gratz Brown upon the ground on the last day, their breaking into and dividing the ranks of the revenue reformers, and carrying off a portion of them to the great hero and advocate of protection—added, of course, always to his own high personal qualities and popularity, and the deep hold he has acquired upon the hearts of the people of the South and the West.

But with his usual perversity of temper and openness to flattery, Mr. Greeley will probably continue to give his faith and attribute his success to those who fawn upon him that they may use him, and to slander and abuse those braver and truer friends who dare expose these creatures to him and the world, and tell him the truth that he needs to hear, even if he does not like it.

Watterson, in the *Courier-Journal*, May 6, came to the support of the Springfield political writer's comment. "Mr. Greeley will do well to read it and consider it. He has no better friend than Mr. Bowles; and . . . all that Mr. Bowles says about Governor Fenton is true."

Horace White, on May 4, 1872, produced a more modern example of the combination of reporter and editorialist. "The nomination of Mr. Greeley," his dispatch to the Chicago *Tribune* began, "was accomplished by the people, against the judgment and strenuous efforts of the politicians—using the latter word in its larger and higher sense."

Great men, Byron observed, lived before Agamemnon, and other bards have acquainted us with the fact that great men lived after Helen's formidable brother-in-law was murdered by his queen and her paramour. Before the Quadrilateral there were Junius, Philip Freneau, Peter Zenger, Thomas Jefferson, and the gifted authors of the Federalist Papers. After the Quadrilateral, perhaps the first editorial commentator to qualify for membership in this high company was E. L. Godkin of the New York *Evening Post* and the *Nation*.

Most of his comment, which moved and shook his era, was unsigned. But this then current practice of anonymity was neither intended to conceal, nor did it conceal, the identity of the writer.

I have chosen these excerpts from his works in the daily and periodical press to support my rating of Godkin, which is the rating of his contemporaries and those who since have acquainted themselves with his product.

The following is Godkin at his indignant best, and never has there been better. Among his favorite topics were foreign policy and the deficiencies of President Cleveland. In the *Evening Post* and in the *Nation*, from 1892 to 1898, Godkin displayed his powers at their fullest in the following comments:

We began the process of alienating and irritating the Chileans by the appointment of Egan as our Minister—in itself contemptuous to the verge of insult. We continued it by open displays of sympathy with Balmaceda during the Civil War; by our seizure and pursuit of the Itata, in disregard of the law laid down by our State Department; by permitting our naval officers during four months to sneer at, abuse, defy, and threaten the Chileans, with the permission or approval of our Navy Department and the loud encouragement of our Government press. When the riot occurred, we forced on the Chileans, with an absolute disregard of the decencies of diplomatic intercourse, a view of governmental responsibility for mob violence which we had ourselves a short time previously utterly repudiated. (*Evening Post,* Jan. 29, 1892)

It is very difficult to say anything intelligent about abandoning Samoa, without knowing more than the world generally knows about our reasons for going there. It would probably never have entered into the head of anyone in this country to go near the islands if some German traders had not established themselves there early in the Seventies, and begun to meddle

in native politics, and appropriate native property, and call
in German men-of-war when they got into quarrels with the
people they were robbing. Their proceedings were so high-
handed that they soon got into collision with the American
consul, and his complaints had to be noticed. The natives are
split up into factions, and are apparently incapable of carrying
on a regular government. If this be so, the proper persons to
take possession of it or "protect" it are the Australians. It is
in their "system." It is nearer to New Zealand than any other
civilized state, and is in the direct line of their communication
with the rest of the world. But instead of proposing this we
entered into a tripartite treaty in 1889 with Germany and
England for the establishment of an independent government
under foreign advice and assistance. It has not worked well.
The islands are still rent by disputes and faction fights, and
life and property are reported to be insecure. One of the worst
questions arises out of the land titles. The land of the islands
has for many years been going steadily to the Germans and
other foreign traders, and the natives feel they have been
cheated out of it. In fact, if we substitute traders for mission-
aries, the case of Samoa is very like that of Hawaii. The traders
have got the land and the kings are undoubtedly unchaste.
(*Evening Post,* May 17, 1894)

We never have the smallest difference with a foreign power,
when our newspapers and some of our public men do not *at
once* begin to talk of an appeal to arms, to count our ships
and guns, to accuse the other side of "arrogance and insult,"
and "mendacity," and "hypocrisy," and "deceit," and to assure
the President of the Support of Congress in case he should
immediately resort to hostilities. (*Evening Post,* March 17,
1892)

. . . on Friday and Saturday he [Cleveland] was overwhelmed
with the execrations of business men; on Sunday he received
the most unanimous and crushing rebuke that the pulpit of

the country ever addressed to a President. He made his appeal
to the conscience of the mob; he has now heard from the conscience of the God-fearing people, and their judgment upon
him leaves him morally impeached of high crimes and mis-
demeanors.

Mr. Cleveland says now just what Debs said in the summer
of 1894. Law or no law, Debs and his fellow-anarchists gloried
in being "masters of the situation." It is a melancholy thing
to find the President who put them down with a firm hand,
now displaying himself as the greatest international anarchist
of modern times. (*The Nation,* Dec. 26, 1895, p. 456)

This is the time to say a last word about "yellow journalism." Two weeks hence people will probably think no more
about it. Well, what we have to say is that every week furnishes
illustrations of the extent to which the public is responsible
for the very evil which it is the fashion to deplore so much
and denounce so much, in conversation. Everyone who knows
anything about "yellow journals" knows that everything they
do and say is intended to promote "sales". . . or, in other
words, is meant to be an advertisement of the paper and show
the power of "journalism." Therefore, they are always trying
to do something queer and big, so as to attract attention and
sell more copies. Predictions of war and reasons why war is
inevitable are of the same mental and moral value as puffs of
shoes or of quack medicines. Insofar, therefore, as these papers
are public evils and a national disgrace, to be got rid of if
possible, the best service any man can render to the state is
to refuse to aid and abet them in any schemes for attracting
notice to themselves. Yet how few men, however highly placed,
there seem to be who are capable of this trifling act of patriotism. No one—absolutely no one—supposes a yellow journal
cares five cents about the Cubans, the Maine victims, or anyone else. A yellow journal office is probably the nearest approach, in atmosphere, to hell, existing in any Christian state.

In gambling-houses, brothels, and even in brigands' caves there is a constant exhibition of fear of the police, which is in itself a sort of homage to morality, or acknowledgment of its existence. In a yellow journal office unscrupulousness and deviltry, far from hiding themselves, boast themselves, and are puffed up. Consequently, whatever a yellow journal does, whether it gets up an enterprise of art, or charity or amusement, is done as an advertisement simply, that is, to call attention to what it has for sale in the nature of deviltry. Nevertheless, when one of them offers a yacht voyage, with free wine, rum, and cigars, and a good bed, under the guise of philanthropy, or gets up a committee for holy purposes, and promises to puff it, it can get almost anyone it pleases to go on the yacht voyage and serve on the committee—Senators, lawyers, divines, scholars, poets, presidents, and what not. All have "patriotism" enough to help the government to fight the Spaniards, but only a few the little bit necessary to refuse consent when sinners entice them. They continue to promote in this way the prosperity of this awful public disgrace. (*Evening Post,* March 17, 1898)

For fifty years and more, Watterson's hold on a national audience was so firm and constant that, in exposition of my thesis, I am obliged once more to borrow from his writings.

In 1916, at the time of the national conventions, though nearing eighty, Watterson decided to transfer some of his editorial comment to the news columns of the *Courier-Journal.* This required him to leave his quiet retreat in the country and write in the office at midnight, against the deadline. Under the alternate headings of "The Front" and "The Situation," he analyzed and impaled my news dispatches as they came in from Chicago. And plain in the subjoined is that Watterson availed himself of the extra latitude that comes to a news commentator who also makes the policy of the paper—a function now discharged only indirectly by those whom publishers have granted the privilege by forfeit.

With his one good—and fierce—blue eye a few inches from the copy paper, and writing a caligraphy that baffled all but one printer in the *Courier-Journal* composing room, Watterson loosed his full artillery on Theodore Roosevelt and the Republicans in these signed editorial comments in June 1916:

It is impossible to deal with the situation at Chicago, made up almost exclusively out of clashing personalities and rival interests and ambitions, without seeming to take sides.

Thus, for example, might be cited the conviction of the Courier-Journal that Theodore Roosevelt can never again be elected President of the United States. As a Democrat, we ought to work for and welcome his nomination. But before all partyism we put the public welfare. The Teddy mania is a disease. It is a disease to be diagnosed as half hysteria and half treason. The Roosevelt candidacy is a revolt against American institutions and traditions. His nomination would put the seal of a great party upon this revolt. His methods are Mexican, not American. His Americanism is the rankest electioneering clap-trap. We would spare the country the wrench of a campaign having life-tenure for its paramount issue; we would save it from the implication, and the world assumption, that Republican Government in America is a failure.

Our belief is that the Republican party can elect no nominee this year; but it may have a future; and, sinner though it is and has been, we would not damn it to the eternity of discredit which would surely follow its surrender to a conspiracy to Mexicanize the Republic and Diazify the Presidency.

No man, however great, is essential to the prowess and glory of this nation; nor party either, for the matter of that. Neither can the people be saddled and bridled and ridden by the organized wealth of the country embarked upon the personal fortunes of any popular hero seeking power at the expense of free institutions. Only a few, a very few, and they the nouveaux riches, and certain of the corporations, are yet ready for the Man-on-Horseback.

The Situation at Chicago may be summed up in a few brief sentences; Harding's plea for harmony, though eloquent, fell on deaf ears; there is nothing but crimination and recrimination; confusion and anger; the weather adding its inclemency to the desolation of some, the despair of others, of the Republican leaders. Bluff is the word on one side, dogged patience on the other, with the assurance of the nomination of the Justice unless he takes himself out of it. Says a private wire [mine] to the Editor of the Courier-Journal: "No tangible harmony development today or to-night. The Hughes men will proceed to nominate him on an early ballot; the Bull Moose will nominate Roosevelt Friday. The conventions may then appoint conference committees to confer with Roosevelt and Hughes. The Platform Committee is just killing time to avoid framing a preparedness plank until they know what Roosevelt and Hughes want and are going to do. The Situation is back to last Sunday night except that the desire to win is more intense; that's all. No one can anticipate results. The New York and Chicago papers are not even trying."

"Failing to light his pipe with his bootjack," says Bulwer-Lytton of John Burley, "he began to weep," and in like manner the two Chicago conventions, failing to attain harmony through the agency of the Big Stick, turn to platform making.

It is parlous work. Platforms have been always more or less springes to catch woodcock. Latterly they seem made to be disregarded. Their promises are taken, therefore, by serious people as lightly "as dicers' oaths, or lovers' vows."

Thus far the proceedings at Chicago, equally with the

94

weather, put a damper upon the hearts alike of men and women; a chill upon enthusiasm; a blight upon hope. At the Auditorium [Bull Moose] all is noise and bluff; at the Coliseum [Republican] silence and "shuffle the cards." So they mark time; they doze and drone; they saw wood and say nothing, or next to nothing, as they listen to the mournful music of the surging lake and the brass bands playing "the tune the old cow died of."

The goose to be cooked being the people and the platform the three "P's"—Preparedness, Protection and Patriotism— furnish the stuffing. According to the Colonel he is the only American. The rest of us are half-breeds. In the matter of preparedness the only original Jacob lives at Oyster Bay. As for the Tariff he would build it as high as the skies—"to the Moon, by gad, sir!" And, meekly, their ear to the telephone, the slumbering braves and sleeping beauties of the Coliseum listen for wisdom and more wisdom from the Sage of Saga-more Hill; only they dare not nominate the Colonel. " 'Tis strange, 'tis passing strange! 'Tis pitiful, 'tis wondrous piti-ful!" The poor, old G.O.P.! To such base uses may be come at last.

Like the gentleman who did not believe in ghosts because he had seen so many of them, the Courier-Journal does not believe in party platforms. Any fool can make a party platform, and it is a cold day when any old platform cannot be twisted to serve the turn of any old party. Presently the Democratic clans will meet at St. Louis. Do the dickey birds at Chicago imagine that the Democrats will have no platform? Sure! And what it will do to the flag and the footlights and the hosspistols! —shove the growler this way, and the hot dog, and don't everybody speak at once! (*Courier-Journal,* June 9, 1916)

Beginning in about the second decade of this century, the field of signed editorial comment was occupied, and, because of the new process of syndication, was dominated, by three men of talents that would be rated exceptional now as then. They were Frank L. Simonds, whose analyses and recommendations as to foreign affairs have not been surpassed; Sir A. Maurice Low, whose column in the *World*—"A Looker-On in Washington"—would have confronted Junius with a rival in his time; and Mark Sullivan. First, as editor of *Collier's*, Sullivan regularly wrote the "Comment on Washington" that influenced men and affairs in the United States, and then, as a syndicated columnist, he produced for many years a continuation of this column from the better observation post of the Capital itself.

I shall begin with Low.

Washington, Jan. 1—Day by day in every way the Association [League] of Nations becomes thinner and thinner.

In midsummer, 1920, it was rotund and dimpled. All the reports were quite cheerful. Given daily injections of serum 31, compounded by the most eminent specialists, it waxed lusty. Day by day in every way it became more beautiful. Its fond and adoring parents were the envy of all. Its numerous devoted sisters and cousins and aunts, not to mention grandparents and godfathers and godmothers, shared in the universal joy. Thirty-one great men, the greatest men in the whole world, watched the dear little thing grow and grow and knew the time would soon come when it would confound its enemies.

Now alas! our fond hopes have been dashed. We have fallen upon evil days. There is no health in the Association of Nations, neither is there strength. Its beauty is no more. Pampered, coddled and watched over, its power to soothe and charm has gone. Once a promise to the weary and distressed, it now brings no comfort to the sorrowful. How things do change once the votes have been counted.

Once upon a time it was considered quite the correct and

proper thing admiringly to talk about the Association of Nations. It was, so to speak, if we may employ the light touch in so grave a matter, the fair-haired boy in a numerous family....

...Grandpapa Lodge was particularly worried, and there were other granddaddies almost as equally disturbed, but none of them quite as much as Grandpa Lodge. He sat in his corner near the fire reading good books and taking a little nap, as old and benevolent gentlemen are apt to do after the day's work is done and the reservations safely locked up for the night, and he would wake up with a start and see that wretched League of Nations boy making faces at him. It made him angry, and we don't blame him a little bit. That was no way to treat a benevolent grandfather. . . . (*World,* Jan. 2, 1923)

Simonds's was a gentler pen, but it penetrated to the core of his subject. I believe he was the first editorial commentator whose work was published in a number of newspapers comparable to that in which Lippmann and one or two others appear today. And, while his influence cannot be accurately measured, I recall many evidences that it existed and was strong. This was his style in presenting international subjects:

Notwithstanding the obvious gravity of the situation it produced, the Italian incident was welcomed on many sides in Paris with the general comment that it cleared the atmosphere. It induced a situation which must lead to settlement one way or another on many questions. It involved more than any other thing that has yet come up the test of the whole American position in the peace conference.

It should be added, too, before passing to the examination of the issues that the stand of President Wilson was recognized by all Americans and many Europeans alike as a championship, and a powerful championship, of the rights of small people, and it had the approval of those who believed that one of the great purposes of the peace conference is to recognize the rights of these, even when they conflict with the ambitions of the great nations.

In nothing that has been done since he came to Europe has the President more squarely lined up with what Americans conceive to be American ideals than in this particular incident. In the present article I desire to discuss two things: First, the facts that underlie this particular collision and, second, the manner in which this collision is illustrative of the collision between European and American ideas which has marked the whole conference.

The break between the Italians and the President grows out of two wholly dissimilar sets of circumstances—the peculiar domestic situation in Italy itself, and the age-long aspirations of the Italian people to revive the glories of Rome and the conquests of Venice on the eastern shores of the Adriatic. . . .

. . . On the basis of self-determination, Italy has no claim whatever to Dalmatia, and on the basis of the right of nations to free access to the sea, the second of Mr. Wilson's principals, the Jugo-Slavs have a claim to Fiume.

Now, the Italian claim to Dalmatia, that is, to the northern half of Dalmatia, which is alone in question, together with the islands, rests upon the agreement made between Italy and England and France at the moment when she entered the war. As the price of her participation, England and France agreed that Italy should have in addition to the Trentino and Trieste about half of Dalmatia, including most of the islands. At the same time, Fiume was expressly reserved as the port of Austria-Hungary, whose dissolution was not then foreseen.

Italy now demands that her Allies shall fulfill their pledge and they have at all times been ready to agree that Italy should now occupy Dalmatia and annex it. . . . President Wilson, on his part, since the United States was not bound by any such agreement as that to which England and France subscribed, insisted that in accordance with his demand for the self-determination of peoples, Dalmatia should go to Jugo-Slavia. He at the same time insisted that Fiume should be elected into some sort of free port and with a guarantee of the League of Nations thus permit the Slavs to have access to the sea in a manner analogous to the rights assured to the Poles through Danzig. . . .

If the President's method prevails the waning fortunes of the League of Nations will take on new vitality. It will, to a certain degree, have demonstrated the enormous influence of moral as contrasted with military force in the world, for this is precisely the sort of question, of which the Fiume dispute is an example, which must in the future provide tasks for the League of Nations. To all practical purposes the solution the President has now sought, the solution of publishing to the people of the country most affected a statement of a neutral and impartial view of the issues involved, is the method which the League of Nations, when constituted, will undertake. . . .

. . . I think the truth that is coming home to most Americans in Europe now is that, after all, it is impossible to impose American conceptions of European affairs upon Europe or permanently to persuade Europe that American faiths and idealistic solutions, which grow, in part at least, out of American isolation from European problems, can prevail. The growing sense of difference of point of view on all essential questions between the American and the European is one of the most striking circumstances of recent days in the peace conference.

Will the Allies seek to restore great Russia, or, following the German example, strive to divide the Russian Empire of yesterday into half a score of disorganized fragments? More than 250,000,000 of people will be affected immediately by the decision which the conference of Paris has yet to make. Neither the negotiators of the treaties of Westphalia nor the Congress of Vienna faced anything like as grave and complex problems, affecting as many millions of people, as now confront the statesmen gathered here in Paris. In serving their peace terms upon Germany, they have only made a beginning. What is to come may possibly prove ten times as important for the peace of the world. (New York *Tribune,* May 4, 1919)

There is a natural but dangerous tendency to regard the announcement of the terms of peace, so far as they affect Germany, as making the whole settlement of the world and an actual restoration of world peace. The truth is quite otherwise. In dealing with Germany we have imposed a number of economic conditions, a number of military conventions, but so far as Europe is concerned we have only changed the situation of from 6,000,000 to 8,000,000 of people living in approximately 30,000 square miles of territory. There remains before us the task of dealing with territories and populations more than ten times as great.

The future peace of Europe, and therefore of the world, will be possibly even more seriously affected by the decisions we have still to make than any we have reached hitherto. . . .

. . . If we shall in subsequent negotiations, which will liquidate the old Hapsburg and Osmanli empires in Europe, build real states, we shall put seventy millions of liberty loving peoples capable of defending themselves, across the pathway of German expansion. We shall restore the balance of power in Europe, abolished when Russia fell, and we shall do much more. We shall bring satisfaction to millions of people who hitherto have never accepted any European settlement, because no European settlement has taken cognizance of their just rights.

Finally, there is Russia. Many signs point to a rapidly

approaching collapse of Bolshevism, but after Bolshevism, what?

So much for the fact that this is primarily an economic punishment of Germany. Now, in the second place, this peace cannot be a settlement except in the narrowest sense, because it settles nothing. It only arranges a method of settlement. It leaves it for the future to enforce terms. It adjures, in all essential cases with minor exceptions, the liquidation which hitherto has promptly followed war. Therefore, it is impossible now to go beyond the statement that if the terms of peace can be enforced and are enforced it is a just peace. But it may be a generation, granted that Germany does accept the treaty of peace, before anybody can measure its real value.

There is a third circumstance of major importance. The treaty of peace as drafted represents three thoroughly distinct points of view—American, British, Continental. The American point of view was comprehended in the President's insistence on the League of Nations as a basis of peace. The British was comprehended in a dominating desire to preserve and expand Anglo-American friendship, and the only less controlling necessity of preserving intimate association with France as guarantee against possible German aggression in the future. The French point of view was one in which security and reparation were prevailing motives....

...The conflict of these three points of view was immediate, inevitable, and has dominated the whole peace situation. As a result we have a compromise, a compromise to be criticized, as all compromises must be, as a sacrifice of essential principles of all three conflicting elements. Mr. Wilson's American ideal of peace, without bitterness for the future, has been modified almost out of existence by the economic burdens placed upon Germany, burdens which ought of right to be placed upon her, but as they mean long-standing economic servitude of the country, will unquestionably promote as great bitterness as did the annexation of territory in other wars. . . .

The treaty of peace, then—and this is the capital point—is not a settlement. . . . The idea that this is a peace founded on justice is correct, but the idea that this justice, which spells approximate ruin to a great power, will be accepted by it willingly now or in the future is totally false. . . . (Paris, May 11, 1919)

Mark Sullivan wrote in rounder phrases than is the fashion today. And, unlike the wholly editorial commentator, he sought to include in his articles factual material on which to found his opinions. Thus the reporter dominated the editorial writer, and in service to this formula Sullivan sought and presented facts that previously had not been presented, and the clarifying details of facts that had been. I think this is apparent in the following extracts from a column published May 10, 1935:

Washington, May 9—What is being done at Washington is so extraordinary that comparatively few in the country understand it. Writing about it, one has sometimes a futile feeling of inability to describe it in any words that the average man is familiar with. It is alien to the ordinary American's habit of thought as if it were being done in Mars. It is as contrary to what we speak of as common sense as if it were in some fantastically contrived land of topsy-turvy.

And that is just the explanation. Actually, seriously and literally, America is in large part just now a land of topsy-turvy. I do not use that phrase in any comedy sense. A country in which collectivism is the social order and form of government is upside down to a country in which individualism is the social order. What is happening in Washington is that America is being taken from a status of individualism toward one of collectivism. As the successive steps are taken, each new status looks upside-down to eyes familiar with the old. Each new step is a shock to our habitual ways of thinking....

What has happened is this: The government, Triple A, forbade farmers to raise as much cotton as many of them wished to raise, and paid other farmers to plow under cotton already growing. As a result of this and other measures, the price of American cotton is high, foreign consumers buy their cotton from other producing countries, at a world price just now about 10 cents a pound. Because our sales of cotton abroad are falling off seriously, the South is threatened with disaster.

What now does the Administration do? Does it retreat from what it has done about cotton? Not at all.

Looking about, the head of Triple A, Mr. Davis, observes that our exports of automobiles are increasing greatly, about 120 per cent. "There," says Mr. Davis in effect, "there is our answer; the government will control all exports; the government will forbid those automobile manufacturers to sell abroad." If Mr. Davis's proposal is put in terms of addressing Europe, he says in effect, "you must stop buying American automobiles and you must use the money to buy American cotton."

Vaguely one recalls a popular song of the early 1920s: "Yes, we have no bananas, we have no bananas today; We have string beans and onions..."

The New Deal has embarked upon revolution, and to carry it on involves more and more regulation. It is a process in which each step compels another. A process which began in May, 1933, with controlling the raising of cotton, is in May, 1935 at the point where, in order to succeed, it feels it must control the export of automobiles....

In this partial roster of editorial commentators in the United States who have influenced mass opinion and the conduct of public individuals, the names of two shine out with special brilliance. Their national stature grew from the impact of their writings on the readers of the same newspapers in the same city, beginning at about the same time.

Frank Richardson Kent was pre-eminent for many years as a political reporter and commentator. Henry L. Mencken, his friend and colleague on the Baltimore Sunpapers, attained, and held until his death, this pre-eminence in commenting on all aspects of life in the United States and among the members of the human race in general.

Over what must have been the longest period of successful syndication of articles in the history of American journalism, Kent expounded the moves in "The Great Game of Politics" with a gentility, reportorial penetration, honesty, and courage that never were surpassed. And for most of this period (he died several years earlier), Mencken, with the ferocious jocundity of a Rabelais and the withering satire of a Swift, bombarded every sham and shammer in sight from his inexhaustible arsenal of old words launched with incredible precision, and new words that he added to the language.

In selecting the following extract from the massive volume of Mencken's work, the oversigned can hope, within the space restrictions of this essay, only to present glimpses of the personality and talent of this great journalist.

... Government is a thing of men—and under democracy of men palpably inferior and ignominious. Knowing this is very useful. It was not knowing it that exposed the people of America to prohibition.

A long time must elapse, of course, before the lesson soaks in. When no antidote is within reach, the frantic patient is apt to swallow more of the same poison. In the same way the subjects of this great empire, cozened by mountebanks, turn to fresh mountebanks for relief. But they have at least come to suspect that they face mountebanks, and not heroes. The old haloes fall off. Government reveals itself, not as a benign and supermortal power, devoted disinterestedly to the public good, but as a mere camorra of rogues and vagabonds, devoted wholly to their own advantage. On one side stands the dry congressman, wet inside and eager to be wetter. On the other stands the prohibition agent, with his hand out. And in the center stands the ermined judge, judicially tearing up the bill of rights to roll cigarettes.

Such is government, scientifically viewed. Such are the evangelists of law enforcement. I preach no holy war against them. I know of no way, in fact, to get rid of them. But it seems to me there is great advantage in seeing them, at last, exactly as they are—that it is a good and valuable thing to pull them out of their old disguises. Suppose we can't get rid of them at all, now or hereafter? *Soit!* But we may at least avoid the diastrous error of mistaking them for benefactors. We may at least cease mistaking their witless and oppressive orders for divine commands.

Do I exaggerate the stupidity and obliquity of these gentlemen? I think not. Turn to the governors of the American states: there are forty-eight of them. How many show any genuine competence and professional dignity, any honest desire to perform their duties honestly and well, any actual courage, independence and integrity? Certainly not a dozen. Well, then, how many are at the other end of the scale—how many are limber and ignoble Jenkinses, willing and eager to do anything to hold their jobs, to get better jobs—how many have been wet once, became dry, and are now getting damp again? Certainly twice as many. And what will you find in the middle? You will find vacuums, nonentities, blobs.

Turn to the national house of representatives. It consists of nearly 500 men. Of them perhaps forty are of such dignity that it may be said of them that they cannot be bought—not even with votes. Of the forty perhaps a dozen have genuine intelligence. What of the rest? They are absolutely indistinguishable, gathered in plenary session, from a convention of garage keepers. They leap at the word of command, peering this way and that. When there is no command they lie docilely, like dogs upon a hearth rug. It makes little difference where the command comes from: if it is sharp enough, they leap.

The chamber of these abject ciphers is the shrine of government among us. Their absurd proceedings, sufficiently prolonged, result in the enactment of what is called law, and that law we are asked to revere as something almost sacred. Flouting it is not only a breach of decorum; it is an act of treason. If, run amok by fanatics, they decided that we should all wear green neckties, it would become a patriotic duty to wear green neckties. If, run back by other fanatics, they banned green and prescribed red, we should have to change to red.

But isn't law necessary? Of course, it is: who denies it? But it is necessary only when it is necessary. The rest is only insult and oppression, and the citizen is under no more obligation to submit to it than he is to submit to any other insult or oppression. Say I am ill and send for a doctor. He prescribes a dose of Glauber's salts, and I take it without question, for the general experience of man is in favor of it. Moreover, I believe the doctor to be an honest man. But suppose he prescribed, in addition to the Glauber's salts, ten grains of strychnine, a pound of tenpenny nails, and a quart of ground glass? And suppose he pulled out a revolver and ordered me to get his prescription down on penalty of death, and then, having me conveniently stuck up, proceeded to empty my pockets?

This, under the name of government, is what goes on every day. We need laws for certain essential purposes, and we select men to make them for us. Sufficiently urged, they do it. But then they go on to enterprises of their own. They make laws that rob us, laws that annoy and oppress us, laws that deprive us of capital and inalienable rights. They do all this, not mistakenly, but for their private advantage. They forget your business and mine completely, and devote themselves gloriously to their own. And then they try to convince us that what is theirs is really ours—and order us to jail when we protest.

Law enforcement? Go tell it to the marines! (*Chicago Tribune,* Jan. 10, 1926)

Since my design of this chapter automatically excludes contemporaries, and includes only the authors (in any period) of signed and nationally syndicated material, some of the most important and influential editorial commentators have been passed over. If contemporary daily work were being studied, that of David Lawrence would be prominent.

Lawrence has earned a very special rating because he, though responsible also for a great publication and the economy of its employees, has championed the great nineteenth-century liberal tradition in behalf of causes unpopular among those who now call themselves "liberals," but who would suppress the nonconformity true liberalism was established to defend.

And outstanding among the very recently active is the late Anne O'Hare McCormick of the New York *Times.* Were it not for the *Times* policy barring syndication of any material that appears on its editorial page, Mrs. McCormick's contribution to the understanding of world affairs and the trends of American government and daily life would be prominent in this history.

Since the days of the Quadrilateral, American journalism has changed, and mostly for the better. The quality of the news has been greatly improved by the requirement that reporters and desk technicians have special training in science, economics, history, English usage, and the art of government, in the course of a liberal-arts education. The standard of fair play, by which the bias either of reporter or management is hunted down by the news editor for excision from the columns offered to the reader as the honest record of events, has become the standard of most American newspapers. Only in the widespread circulation given by publishers to correspondents who, for keyhole privileges, or because of a congenital "cops and robbers" fixation, gild those news sources which furnish them and blacken those which deny them, does the historic blight of American journalism endure.

As for the editorial commentators, they merely have moved from under the masthead and its suspended province, where alone the awesome "we" is permitted in the expression of judgment, to other parts of the page or the paper, where the personal pronoun denotes they are but individuals. However, their tribe has increased and fabulously prospered.

Statesmen, politicians, administrators, and bureaucrats hang on the pronouncements of the tribe, and sometimes this brings about changes in policies and reversals or modifications of actions contemplated or taken. Syndication has enriched some commentators beyond the power or inclination of individual publishers to pay them the over-all wage which, prorated among hundreds, provides each customer with stylish, high-quality goods at a very moderate cost.

This affluence, which even predecessors who owned or partly owned their papers did not approximate, has made the Washington residences of these fortunate few the centers of gracious and lavish hospitality for the entertainment of the most prominent news makers here and abroad. Invitations to these functions are highly prized, and the hosts develop a flattering intimacy with the great and the near-great that frequently yields information which lends special accuracy and authority to their comment on the news.

These few, even fewer from the new journalism of radio and television, also reap the reward of membership in the secretly assembled, very special groups, usually selected by Ernest K. Lindley of *Newsweek,* in which, over a good dinner, the most inaccessible or cautious officials and politicians "tell all."

The effectiveness of personal editorial comment as a species of journalism may wane with the glut of the product. For now so much of it appears in the morning or evening paper that one is beginning to hear more often the ominous remark: "I read such-and-such in the *Blank,* but I can't remember who wrote it." Also, confusion is spread when the galaxy of oracles in a single newspaper dispute, as they do frequently, over both facts and conclusions.

But there is a quality in Lippmann's writing and thinking that impresses its source on the memories even of the most omnivorous consumers of editorial comment. His colleagues at home and abroad read Lippmann with unique fidelity and respect; he is their foremost clarifier of complicated issues, and their acknowledged master of the prose of interpretative journalism. Hence his special influence on the contemporary scene.

VI

The Columnist as Teacher and Historian

BY RAYMOND ARON

In this volume dedicated to our friend Walter Lippmann, I would have liked to have made a comparison between the American columnist and his French equivalent. Unfortunately, such a comparison is impossible for the most obvious of reasons: in France there are no columnists.

Indeed, the columnist, as a kind of sociological-professional phenomenon, if I dare to use the language of the sociologist, seems to me to be defined by two conditions. He does not belong to the staff of a single newspaper, and his articles are published in a number of papers (in newspaper jargon, his articles are syndicated). Neither of these two conditions prevails or is likely to prevail in the foreseeable future in France. Publication in many newspapers requires that none of these newspapers has wide circulation throughout the country. The New York *Herald Tribune* has some readers on the West Coast, but it has a substantial number only on the East Coast and particularly in and around New York City. Walter Lippmann's articles can be reproduced in a hundred newspapers scattered across the fifty states without interfering with the sale of the *Herald Tribune* or disturbing the regional readers. There is nothing like this in France. The readers of *Figaro* would be annoyed to find in the local paper the article they had just read in the Paris paper, and they are too numerous for their feelings to be ignored.

The columnist publishes his articles in a large paper, but he is not bound to it as are the regular editorial writers. Neither François Mauriac nor André Siegfried has been part of the editorial team of *Figaro* any more than have I myself. The commentators in *Figaro*, writers, professors, journalists, do not necessarily share the opinions expressed in the unsigned editorials; they do not always adopt the line of the paper. But they cannot express in the articles published under their signatures opinions directly opposite to those of the paper. The French commentator never writes in the newspaper that has the exclusive right to his articles something he does not think, but he does not write all he thinks. If he disagrees on an important problem, he keeps silent or he chooses other outlets—weeklies, monthlies or even books.

Now the risk of disagreement is great, because of phenomena that are probably characteristic not only of France but which may well be more important there than elsewhere. The reader of a book sometimes likes to be surprised or shocked; the reader of a newspaper wants to be justified. If he finds in his newspaper opinions that wound him, he does not cheerfully revise his own convictions. Instead, he becomes indignant at having been betrayed by those whom he had considered his spokesmen. The cancellation of a subscription by an indignant reader is a warning shot to the editor. People often complain that money limits the freedom of the press. The reading public is in many instances more dangerous than money.

Responsible for a commercial enterprise, the editor cannot help but pay attention to the demands of his readers. The conservative, anti-Communist readers in general favor the slogan "Algerie Française." One finds, however, in liberal, middle-class circles and among the intellectuals men who at the same time detest Communists and doubt that France can overcome Algerian nationalism or should undertake to integrate 9,000,000 Moslems into French society. But these men, favoring at the same time the Atlantic alliance and a compromise with Moslem (or Algerian) nationalism, represent only a fraction of the readers. They do not express the emotions of the masses. While they exist among *Figaro*'s readers, they are not large enough in numbers to balance the conformity of the majority. I have published two brochures on Algeria (*The Algerian Tragedy, Algeria and the Republic*). By no means do all of my readers in *Figaro* know that I consider as wrong the policy of pacification carried out without great change by the Fourth Republic and then the Fifth.

On what does the "liberalism" of American editors toward their columnists depend? First, as we have mentioned, it depends on the structure of the press. The columnist, whose articles appear in many newspapers, has a stronger position in relation to the editor of the New York paper than I can have in relation to the editor of the Paris paper. No paper would permit me to say everything I think on every subject. If such-and-such an editor of such-and-such a New York paper disagreed with his opinions, Walter Lippmann could in retaliation find another rostrum. At the same time, we see another reason why the

American editor can be more liberal than the Parisian editor. He knows he is less responsible for the opinions of his columnist than the Parisian editor is for the opinions of his commentator, and he knows that his readers will not confuse him with his columnist.

But in the long run, this distinction is possible only because of a more profound reason. The opposition between the editorials and the columns rarely touches on subjects that inflame the emotions. A columnist can be favorable to a Democratic candidate in a Republican newspaper. Could he be for the integration of schools in a paper that fights for racial segregation? The Algerian questions stir up emotions comparable to those felt by the Southerners rather than feelings similar to those that separate Republicans and Democrats.

Instead of comparing the American columnist and French commentator on the social and professional plane, it seemed to me that another kind of study would suit this book, the study of an obligation common to both. The commentator, especially one who writes about international politics, is able to point up the significance of current events, even the most fleeting, only by reporting the event in connection with the whole background. In its turn, such an interpretation implies a philosophy of history with a dual obligation: a concept of the relationship between sovereign states, and a view of the fundamental problems posed, in our time, by the nature of these states and the redivision of power. Philosopher of history by necessity, the commentator becomes inevitably a teacher. He is forced to explain to his compatriots the kind of world in which they will have to live; what they will have to do in order to help their country survive, prosper, and grow. Walter Lippmann is a political teacher, inspired by a certain philosophy of diplomatic history. It seems to me that the two essays written during the war, *U.S. Foreign Policy* and *U.S. War Aims,* offer a clear and synthesized exposition of this philosophy and make understandable in a larger context the diplomacy the author has recommended during the years since 1945.

In the role of doctrinaire, Walter Lippmann belongs to the school called, in the U.S., "realist," of which Professor Hans Morgenthau is the most systematic interpreter and George F. Kennan the best-known advocate. The states are caught, some against others, in a permanent struggle. Each state's first duty toward its citizens is to assure their collective security, which demands a military force adequate for the obligations undertaken and allies who bring the support needed for security—for there is no security in solitude.

The foreign policy of the United States has been, like that of all countries, determined by considerations of national interest, although American public opinion has not always been aware of it. As Lippmann wrote:

Theodore Roosevelt had, therefore, the elements of a genuine foreign policy. Aware of the American commitments, he sought to develop—though tentatively, unsurely, and without making the matter plain to the nation—the elements of American power: our strategic position by constructing the Panama Canal, our armaments by enlarging the navy, our alliances by adhering to those powers who were our friends and the opponents of our opponents. But these rudimentary beginnings of a true foreign policy were not carried forward by Theodore Roosevelt's successors.

When the United States entered the war in 1917, this decision seemed to American public opinion, in a legalistic, moralistic, idealistic presentation, to be an act of pure generosity. The country believed it was giving without receiving anything in return. "It was made to seem that the new responsibilities of the League flowed from President Wilson's philanthropy and not from the vital necessity of finding allies to support America's vast existing commitments in the Western Hemisphere and all the way across the Pacific to the China Coast."

During the last war, Walter Lippmann, teacher, tried to rectify the concept that his readers might have of the foreign policy of the United States. This differed in appearance more than in reality from that of other powers. The United States had been able to separate itself from world conflicts during the nineteenth century because it had been freely protected by the Royal Navy, and, because of this protection, it had been able to devote itself to the development and colonization of an immense continent. But, in 1917, the security of the United States was threatened by the submarine warfare launched by imperial Germany. "The substantial and compelling reason for going to war was that the cutting of the Atlantic communications meant the starvation of Britain and, therefore, the conquest of Western Europe by imperial Germany." The United States entered the war neither "to make the world safe for all democrats," nor "because it wished to found a League of Nations," but because the security of the United States "demanded that no aggressively expanding imperial power like Germany should be allowed to gain the mastery of the Atlantic Ocean." Failing to understand the meaning and the objectives of the intervention,

American public opinion during the entire period between
the two wars was incapable of conceiving or even of sus-
taining any coherent diplomacy, swinging between an
impossible isolation and a universal juridical order equally
impossible. Finally, in the summer of 1939, the Committee
on Foreign Relations of the Senate recommended at the
same time the abrogation of the commercial treaty with
Japan and the nonabrogation of the embargo on the pur-
chase of arms by France and Great Britain. To create
enemies without giving oneself arms to combat them with
and without assuring oneself of allies, this was the tragic
result of the refusal to recognize foreign policy for what
it was.

Having denounced the errors of the past, how did Walter Lippmann see the world after the war? (We omit the
problem of the Pacific, which has been fundamentally
changed by the victory of the communists in China.)
Walter Lippmann's concept is defined, first, by a triple
negation: neither return to isolation, nor crusade for
democracy, nor peace based on a League of Nations. The
relations between states are a rivalry of power; peace can
be based only on a balance of strength. This balance, in
our time, can be established only through alliances, or,
better, through regional communities. While the battle
was raging, Walter Lippmann was teaching his compatriots the permanent necessity of the Atlantic community.
"We can be certain of the nations which are indispensable
members of the Atlantic community. They are Great
Britain and France in Western Europe, the United States
and Canada in North America."

The Atlantic community, as Walter Lippmann described
it more than fifteen years ago, differs in many points from

the Atlantic alliance as it has since been constituted. The community included the states of South America, while the Atlantic alliance is more limited. But the difference is more apparent than real. The center of the Atlantic community was the military alliance of the United States, Great Britain, and France, an alliance existing today. While the states of the British Commonwealth, of Central and South America, of Western Europe, which Walter Lippmann included in this community, belong, some to the Atlantic alliance, others to another network of American alliances, all live in fact inside the oceanic system, participating in the "good neighbor principle."

World order can be founded only on a number of regional communities. The basic problem appeared in 1942, as it does in 1959, to be that of coexistence between the Atlantic community and the other regional communities, particularly that called the "Russian Orbit." "Quite evidently the crucial question of how long and how confident can be the peace after this war will be determined by the maintenance of the alliance between the Russian Orbit and the Atlantic Community. Whether there is to be a third world war in the twentieth century depends upon whether the Russians come to rest within their orbit, the Atlantic States in theirs, and whether they then concert their policies towards Germany and Japan." Basically, this question remains unanswered, although the arms of massive destructive power create between war and peace the possibility of a third condition, the "cold war," determined by the absence of an accepted international order and the refusal of an armed conflict.

Walter Lippmann was fully aware that a world order, thanks to the coexistence of regional communities, is not compatible with every policy carried out by the dominant power inside its sphere of influence. A certain policy adopted by Russia toward her neighbors would inevitably bring about a conflict with the Atlantic community. "A Russian policy of aggrandizement in Europe, one which threatened the national liberties of her neighbors, would inexorably be regarded as such a threat to Britain and America that they would begin to encourage the nations which resisted Russia." In other words, the little nations of Eastern Europe cannot count on the help of the United States and Great Britain to assure their safety. Their only chance is to arrive at an agreement with the Soviet Union which, in the interest of its own safety and of world peace, will be satisfied with friendship and will not demand the submission of the small neighboring states.

The plurality of regional communities is today an accomplished fact, but it does not constitute coexistence. Does this mean that events have proved Walter Lippmann wrong? Before this question can be answered it must be shown that the events of the war could have left another heritage. Our friend saw clearly that the fate of the states of Eastern Europe would decide the relations between the Atlantic community and the Soviet sphere. He stated as an indisputable fact that the sea powers were incapable of assuring the liberty of the states next to the Soviet Union. He then concluded that the only hope was that the Soviet Union might be contented with the neutralization "in the realm of power politics" of these states. "Does this mean that Poland, the Danubian states and the Balkan states have no prospect of assured independence and that they are destined inexorably to become satellites of Russia or to be incorporated into the Soviet Union? The question cannot be answered categorically at this time." In other words, he was not sure that the states of Central and Eastern Europe could belong to the Soviet sphere of influence without being sovietized, and he was sure that the sovietization of these states would mark the rupture of the war alliance with the Soviet Union and the beginning of a third world war. These are the fears of yesterday, not the hopes that have become realities.

The primary war aim of the United States in Europe was, Walter Lippmann wrote, to prevent Germany from "holding the balance of power in Europe." What does this mean? The central idea was as follows. Any attempt on the part of the West to use Germany militarily to oppose the Soviet Union would be condemned to failure. In a competition between the Soviet Union and the West to win the military co-operation of Germany, the West would be the loser in advance because the Soviet Union has much more to offer than the West. The only solution would be the following:

In the end, it seems to me, a disarmed Germany can come safely and properly to rest within the international exchange economy of the Atlantic community. But Germany can be so placed only with the sincere consent of the Soviet Union. Therefore, there must be no question of Germany's being included in the military system of the Atlantic power. By making a demilitarized Germany dependent on the seaborne commerce the best guaranty will be provided that the age-long German expansion to the east, the *Drang nach Osten*, is ended.

Perhaps the reader will be astonished to recall formulas which, however reasonable they might have seemed at that time, have been made obsolete by intervening events, in particular by the division of Germany into two states. But, indeed, the basic formula is still valid. Walter Lippmann does not believe that either of the two camps agrees that all Germany could belong militarily to the other alliance. The military neutralization of Germany is still, in his eyes, the only peaceful solution, one which separates the Atlantic community from the Russian Orbit without threatening the vital interests either of the Atlantic world or the Soviet sphere.

To this concept of the problem, Walter Lippmann has remained faithful through the fourteen years that have elapsed since the unconditional surrender of the Third Reich. He has never approved of the Western policy toward Germany, inspired by the United States. He has, through the weeks and years, multiplied his expressions of doubt, reserve, criticism. The profound reasons for this attitude stem from the preceding analysis. Germany cannot remain divided indefinitely. In the contest going on between the Russian Orbit and the Atlantic community, it is the Russian Orbit that has the best chance, the most telling arguments, for convincing the Germans that they have the means to return to them the unity to which they most aspire above everything else.

Many times, Walter Lippmann has believed that the rulers at Bonn were about to negotiate with those of Pankow. As soon as Chancellor Adenauer's authority had been firmly established, Lippmann recognized that the eventuality, always inevitable in his eyes, of an agreement between the two Germanies, had been postponed. But he thought that Chancellor Adenauer's successors will someday do what he, up to now, has refused to do. Thus we arrive at the present crisis, brought on by the Russian threats against Berlin, since obviously the Westerners cannot leave Berlin without a balancing concession from Russia and the Russians cannot accept indefinitely in West Berlin a Western presence that prevents the stabilization of the communist regime in East Germany. The only solution is a global negotiation, at a minimum on some form of disengagement, at most on the unification of a Germany without military ties with either of the two camps. Walter Lippmann does not deny the extreme difficulty of this negotiation and, even more, of a conceivable agreement. But according to his philosophy of foreign policy, he thinks the chances of an agreement are greater than I am inclined to.

In his eyes, the rulers of the Soviet Union, like those of Germany (or of the Germanies) are, in the final analysis, in the long view, first Russians and Germans, not communists and anticommunists. The national interest of Russia lies not in absorbing Germany, but in neutralizing it in order to be separated from the Atlantic community by a buffer zone. The national interest of Germany lies in the reconstitution of German unity. The national interest of France, Great Britain, and even the United States is to have a Germany that is neither a prize nor an arbiter, that does not risk creating the occasion for a conflict feared by all. In this perspective, all national interests would be served by the unification of a neutral Germany.

Why is this solution, the best on paper, so difficult to achieve at this point? Why does it meet with so much skepticism? It is because it implies, first, a progressive harmony between the two regimes (economic, social, political) of the East German Republic and the Federal Repub-

lic; then a separation between the political-military status
and the economic-social status. It is true that this second
need was satisfied in the case of Austria, which is, diplo-
matically and militarily, neutral, while belonging, in the
fields of economics, culture, and institutions, to the West.
The question is whether what is possible for a little country like Austria is equally possible for a big country like
Germany. In Austria, the Russian authorities never tried
to sovietize their occupation zone. In East Germany, the
union between the Socialist party and the Communist
party, a preliminary to sovietization, took place in 1946.
Is a liquidation of the communist zone compatible with
the interests, not of eternal Russia, but of a Russia whose
leaders consider themselves interpreters of a revolutionary
movement with universal aspirations? Eternal Germany is
interested, above all, in unity, but the leaders of Pankow,
like those of Bonn, are interested, above all, in maintain-
ing the circumstances to which they owe their power.

While granting that the two camps are interested in a
unified and neutral Germany, one must also realize that
they both fear that this unified Germany might slide from
one side to the other. Thus, each must demand a reciprocal agreement, along with unification, with guarantees as
absolute as possible against the eventuality either of sovietization or of a reattachment to the West. Is it possible to
imagine guarantees efficacious at the same time against the
former and the latter? Simple disengagement raises a
world of problems. Would the demilitarization or semi-
demilitarization of a zone in Germany and in the center of
Europe be acceptable to the West if it were accompanied
by the political *status quo*? And is not the maintenance of
communist regimes where they are established one of the

principles of soviet diplomacy? Following this line of thought, one would oppose the buffer-zone theory of Walter Lippmann with the idea of the division of the contested countries; the division being a substitute for the buffer zone when the conflict is ideological as well as military.

Besides, no one has shown better than our friend, in a period when so many others have been deceived by war propaganda, the roots of a possible conflict among the former allies of the war against the Third Reich. Lippmann writes: "This persistent evangel of Americanism in the outer world must reflect something more than meddlesome self-righteousness. It does. It reflects the fact that no nation, and certainly not this nation, can endure in a politically alien and morally hostile environment; and the profound and abiding truth that a people which does not advance its faith has already begun to abandon it." And, at another moment in *U.S. War Aims*, Lippmann explained at what point a universal society must demand a human bill of rights. We must, he wrote, speak to the Russians and ask them to rally to the cause of democratic liberty across the world.

The proof that they have accepted they alone can give—in the measures they take when the war is over, to validate their own constitutional promises, and to make free, equal and reciprocal the exchange of news and opinions between their own people and their present allies. If they refuse, we can still do our very best to get on with them, persisting through the ordinary channels of diplomacy in the effort to prevent a third World War. But if they refuse, it will be better not to deceive ourselves, and to become relaxed in the semblance, which will have little reality, of a universal society for the maintenance of peace.

Such has been for a long time the state of world affairs. The regional systems were developed. They are hostile to each other. They are incapable of defining a world order for lack of essential agreement. The world organization, as Walter Lippmann feared, is "a forum in which differences are accentuated by public debate and agreement obstructed because they call for public compromises which appear humiliating."

To forestall a third world war there remains only the wisdom of the old diplomacy. How far can it go in this period of mass societies and ideologies? Can it arrange a territorial solution in Europe, acceptable to the two camps, or can it keep the conflict within the limits of the cold war until the day when, on one side or the other, some of the main facts will have been fundamentally modified?

VII

The Logic of Allied Unity

BY IVERACH McDONALD

Cast your bread upon the waters. The journalist does that every day of his life, with each article that goes off into the streets and trains and homes. He is assured that the bread will return after many days. Yet all of us know the misgivings and frustrations while waiting for even a faint sign that some of our work has landed anywhere. If there is a mistake in it, of course, we know from the moment of the first telephone call and are constantly reminded of it throughout the day. But how often, when after long discussions we have given of our best and produced an argument which is, we believe, logical, illuminating, new, and constructive, no bells ring at all. One or two experts, met by chance some days later, may commend the article a little hazily. Or the editor may get a letter—very late, when the article is already outdated by events—from a friend in a distant embassy. But, as for influencing action, it is like dropping a stone down a well and waiting in vain for a splash or rattle at the bottom; nothing but silence. At times, a rough-and-ready rule seems to apply. The sounder and newer the thought, the greater the silence in response. One may be consoled by the experience of a Scottish professor I knew. He said that he had always to repeat any really new point three times before his students, at the third telling, seized on it in the light of surprise and discovery. Yet very often in journalism, even after the fifth or tenth telling, there seems nothing to show at all.

It may seem extremely odd that such dismal reflections appear when so many of us are saluting Walter Lippmann, pre-eminent as a political analyst and commentator. But it is not really odd. The reflections are not out of place. Walter Lippmann's work, by its very excellence over so long a time, forces to the forefront the question of the role and the effectiveness of the serious journalist, whether editor or columnist, in influencing public opinion and public events. We puzzle our brains over policies each day. We write. But to what end? With what result? Is it water over the dam?

Many believe that the day of the serious journalist is fading. They say that the role of the editor, the analyst, the leader-writer, the columnist declined step by step as the old Utilitarian beliefs were shown up as inadequate in explaining the working of modern democracy. We all remember the Utilitarians' confidence that the dawn of the Enlightenment and the spread of popular education would put an end to irrational beliefs and all men would thereby be freed to see clearly, and to pursue their own best interests. Hence it followed, with almost mathematical certainty, that if the people's representatives were elected by majority vote, the resultant government would produce the greatest happiness for the greatest number. The people's ability to decide where their true happiness lay had, however, to be fortified with knowledge, and it was from the newspaper press that every voter would be able to draw the information on which he could shape his cool and rational judgment. The editor, as Jeremy Bentham said, would be the chairman of a "public opinion tribunal," ensuring that the rival cases of the parties were put fairly to the national jury.

It is easy to smile or weep over the simplicities of the Utilitarian beliefs. Walter Lippmann himself has more thoroughly criticized them in his book *Essays in Public Philosophy*. Yet there were many developments which the most doctrinaire of the philosophers did not and could not foresee. First and foremost, and greatest of all, is the well-nigh fatal tendency of democracies to plump for short-term happiness (or the illusion of happiness) rather than for long-term interest. This tendency was nearly the death of us in the years when we remained disarmed and fondly hopeful in face of German and Japanese rearmament; and it could be the death of us now if we go on giving ourselves more cushions and gadgets ad infinitum rather than facing the needs of the miserably poor countries that are being beguiled by the Communists. There are many reasons for this gravitational pull toward comforts and short-term happiness. It is certainly shown in the growth of the mass-circulation press, with its newspapers of sensation, entertainment, and triviality. Daily reading of fifth-rate stuff, like daily looking at fifth-rate programs on television, cannot strengthen powers of judgment. As my own editor, Sir William Haley, said last year:

The climate of a nation's opinions is more important than the opinions themselves. . . . A nation that is continually shown the most familiar aspects of its life as mean, material or trivial will find it harder to face events in a large, moral and serious manner. A nation that is led to believe that, in every activity from sport—particularly sport, for that is something people are sure they really know about—to business and politics, favour, self-interest and cupidity rule the roost will not long acquiesce in its leaders acting even in particular cases in a disinterested and far-seeing manner. It is a grave mistake, therefore, to discount and cease to care about the standards and philosophy of the popular Press. No matter what the record may show about its ineffectiveness in swaying general elections, no matter what the pundits may say about any particular lack of influence, I believe that the climate of opinion is, in the long run, largely in its hands.[1]

The moment, however, that one becomes thoroughly depressed about the trade in general, there comes much more cheering evidence about serious journalism. By a kind of natural rebound from triviality, people are more aware of significant, serious writing when they see it; in Britain, the circulation of the serious newspapers has lately been increasing. And, as news "scoops" have become rarer, articles of original thought and interpretation are thrown into higher relief and, on some days at least, are a newspaper's chief claim to distinction from its rivals. Such articles are read by the core of educated people in each country who are deeply troubled by the impasse between East and West and will turn regularly to a trusted newspaper, or an individual writer, for elucidation and suggestions. The long world crisis has been a testing time for brains, and only the hardest, the steadiest, the most

[1] The Formation of Public Opinion. Being the Twenty-Fifth Haldane Memorial Lecture, delivered at Birkbeck College, March 11, 1958.

resourceful, and the bravest (like Walter Lippmann's) have survived unscathed in their readers' estimation. In journalism, almost anyone can turn out old thoughts on new subjects. It takes a big man to go on producing new thoughts on old subjects.

Yet to what end? With what results? The first disturbing questions have to be faced. The serious articles very seldom have a direct impact on popular thinking or feeling. To the public as a whole, it is often as though they had not been written. Some of the most excellent articles, let us face it, have no discernible effect anywhere, being written much too ahead of the climate of opinion or much too late, when policy is already launched. The other articles, the fortunate ones, usually have their impact by influencing the comparatively few men who influence events. They operate through the Establishment, if you like, provided it is understood that the Establishment includes not only the government or the administration, but the leaders of the opposite party and the trade unions. The articles operate, to put it another way, along the grapevine, among the political leaders, the administrators, the heads and tutors of colleges, the industrialists, the labor leaders. No other single journalist, working on his own, has had so great an effect over so long a period as Walter Lippmann.

The effect is seen especially on Anglo-American relations. To spell it out more fully, Walter Lippmann's books and articles have, without any doubt at all, helped enormously—at times decisively—the cross-fertilizing process of thinking on the world dilemma that goes on the whole time between influential groups in the United States and Britain. Even to talk of groups goes too far. It is not so much a matter of "the thinking in government circles" or "feeling among opposition ranks." It is, rather, what the Society of Friends calls the "sense of the meeting," the highest common factor of serious thought among some men within the government, some within the opposition, among officials, and in politically educated circles outside; sometimes this highest common factor swings to the government side, sometimes against it. Either way, it becomes a pressure on policy, even when that pressure is for a long time resisted.

Looking back on journalistic work of ten, fifteen, twenty years ago is often unflattering to the work. Wrong deductions stand out. Bold, new, successful leads to thought tend now to appear mild and platitudinous. That is simply because, being well-judged and well-directed, they have been overtaken by the events which they foreshadowed and have been submerged in the general climate of opinion that they helped to form. It is hard now to recall, for example, that when Walter Lippmann published his *U.S. Foreign Policy* in 1943, the very title of the book was challenging and revolutionary, postulating the need for an active American foreign policy after the years of withdrawal. Even more challenging was his recognition of an inevitable Anglo-American alliance within a broad "Atlantic Community." All this, as I remember, had a bracing and heartening impact on those British people who were trying to look ahead to the world that would have to be shaped after victory, and were wondering whether America would swing back to isolation. The following year, in 1944, there came the second challenge, in *U.S. War Aims*, in which Walter Lippmann dismissed all the visionary plans for setting up a European federation. He was quite sure, for one thing, that Germany would dominate such a federation, and one of the primary war aims should, rather, be to make it as impossible for Germany to hold the balance of power in Europe as for Japan to hold it in East Asia. But all such thoughts—for keeping Germany disarmed and, his other one, for establishing a neutralized belt of states in Eastern Europe—necessarily depended on the maintenance of the wartime alliance among the United States, Britain, and Russia. Without such continuation of partnership, the world (it was obvious to Walter Lippmann, as to everyone else) would be shaping for a third and greater war. Looking back, we can all say a little loftily that he was wrong—so were many others at the time—in imagining that Poland, Romania, and the rest could be neutralized and Germany kept disarmed. Many were too slow to recognize that Russia would also want a regional pact, covering the East European lands across which she had been invaded. But it is fair to remember that there were many Russian diplomatists of high rank in those years who saw clearly enough the evils and dangers that would come from dividing Europe. Several in Moscow, especially in 1945, told me how anxious they were as they saw the "untold difficulties and dangers ahead." They hoped, even then, that Russia and the Western powers might co-operate in establishing in European countries something that they called "economic democracy," something between capitalism and Russian socialism, and in that way avert the rigid division into two camps. I recall this simply to show that some thinking on co-operational lines was going on in Moscow as the war ended. So Western hopes of some partnership were not wholly baseless. But the Russians who were thinking that way were swept aside by Stalin with the results we know.

"Friendly governments" in Eastern Europe meant governments whose friendliness to Russia would be guaranteed by the Marxist structure of their states, which in turn would be guaranteed by troops and secret police.

The fatal division was made, it is important to remember, in the years when Britain was still exhausted, still crippled, still unable to pay her way, after her struggles and spendings during the war. When one traveled through Europe in those early years after the war, one was continually besought that Britain "should give a lead" somehow, somewhere. Opportunities were plain enough to see. But how could we give a lead when we needed great help ourselves even to keep going? They were the years when Ernest Bevin used to say that his whole foreign policy would be different if he had some coal to export, and when he had to tell Washington that we could no longer keep up our commitments to Greece, still beset with the civil war. None of us in Britain like looking back on that dark time, but it is necessary to do so to understand what it meant to us then to have stalwart and undoubting friends in the United States; and what it meant when the Marshall Plan, which Walter Lippmann had advocated for so long, and the Atlantic alliance took on life. Britain and Western Europe were out of the slough at last. And, on the other side, within a few years, Stalin was dead (March 1953). It was then that the debate was taken up again— how can we live together if we are not to blow ourselves up?—and it has never stopped.

This unending debate, this tense tussle between the two world camps, opens up a large question for journalists. It is one that has been little explored. Is serious and independent journalism a help or a hindrance to the Western governments when facing Russia or facing China? Any journalist whose work is widely read and respected, or one who writes in a newspaper that is raked through with a fine comb every day and widely quoted in both camps, has to face the question almost every time he deals with the great issues. The editor and his staff become convinced, for example, that the Western powers are in an untenable or illogical position although they are proclaiming that they will never budge—*e.g.*, the United States and the Chinese offshore islands. Or they see weaknesses in a case that the West is putting forward, with great aplomb, for the tenth time—*e.g.*, the old case for free elections, upheld for so long as the means of uniting Germany. There are countless other examples which spring to mind; some of them are much more debatable in their rights and wrongs than those I have mentioned. The journalist has the compulsion to explain the truth as he sees it. But he knows that, the moment the article appears, expressing his doubts, others will take it up and passages of it will be widely and gleefully quoted, usually out of context, by Moscow or Peking radio. Even if such an incident does not actually stiffen Moscow's or Peking's policy in negotiations (although it may very well do so), it certainly gives them a propaganda advantage. They can say once again that public opinion in the West is against the official Western line. One has to remember, also, that they on their side suffer no such sniping or criticism from a free press. Their case, no matter how extravagant or how soon it is to be revised, remains monolithic and unquestioned in each successive stage. Or, to take another example, the editor or individual writer may decide, as talks with Russia are approaching, to set out the Western proposals as he knows them and to suggest possible concessions or compromises to meet any Russian compromises. Very often, because he has been living with the problem—Germany, say—for months, he can rightly anticipate the Western moves. A moan of anguish goes up from the Western diplomatists, who say that the newspaper has exposed their hand before they have had time to play it. Meanwhile, once again, the Russians keep their own cards close to their chests. Yet again, every journalist has, many times in his career, been begged to play down or not to write on allied differences, especially if they have not yet come to the surface. (A recent example was when General de Gaulle put forward his plans for reorganizing the NATO commands.) We are told that it will all be quietly buried, that publicity would be fatal, that the full truth is far more complicated and delicate than we imagine, that the great need is to show a united front to the Russians, and so on. Every serious journalist, even the most forthright, has had to decide such questions in his own mind. It is not always easy. He knows only too well that the weapon he holds can fire backward. Experience has shown him how much easier it is to hurt or upset one's friends than one's opponents. That is true in any quarrel; how much truer when Moscow and Peking are armor-plated with a controlled press.

The serious and fundamental answer, of course, is that free comment in the press is one of the liberties on which our way of life is based; it cannot be touched, however embarrassing it may be at times, without invoking other dragooning methods against other liberties of expression. A second answer is that a journalist would not be a journalist unless he believed that, as a general rule, it is better, safer, and more effective in the long run to express differences of view and to expose disputes rather than conceal them and let them fester. He believes that truth can be reached through the open, dialectic process of argument and counterargument. The diplomatist will still say that these answers are all very fine but do not meet his point that articles, whether by Walter Lippmann or anyone else, have sometimes made his negotiations more difficult in recent years and may do so again. What is the journalist's specific answer? Let us admit, for a start, that there are certain times, if negotiations are tense and concentrated, when responsible journalists would hesitate to rock the boat and come out with heavy criticisms of his own side. All of us can recall cases where newspapers, having set out the differences of view, have deliberately withheld comment until a crucial stage has passed. But, apart from such times, no journalist could agree to any limitation on his right to criticize policies or tactics, whether Western or Communist. No one could claim that Western policy in the past few years—say, over Germany or over disarmament—has always been consistent, cogent, and logically watertight or of a kind to be negotiable. Even a united Western press would not have made the Russians sign on the dotted line. And we know with equal certainty that a wrong course, unless corrected, is apt to become more wrong, more sterile, or more dangerous. These are justifications for speaking out. The diplomatist, however, will come back by saying that a journalist, however talented, cannot hope to know as much as those who are in the game. In other words, a journalist, working in his office or study, traveling a part of the year, meeting diplomatists and politicians and businessmen, can amass a good deal of information on which to form a judgment, yet he cannot hope to rival the detailed information at the disposal of his government. That is perfectly true. But in formulating its policy, a government has often to shorten sail, and tack and turn, because of electoral, parliamentary, or congressional calculations, because of considerations of prestige, and, most of all, because of the need to make adjustments to keep the allies in line. So the end result is often very different from the original plan; in fact, only a pale reflection of it, and no one at heart has much confidence in it. The journalist has not made "negotiations more difficult" when he has pointed out that the emperor has no clothes. Mr. Khrushchev and his experts could see that for themselves. Without implying—far from it—that the journalist is always right, I do suggest that there are some quite objective reasons, because he is less caught up in the pressures that often inhibit or distort policy, why he can sometimes put out a simpler and clearer case than the diplomatists. Admittedly this can be embarrassing to our negotiators. Yet I cannot myself think of any negotiations in recent years in which a Western proposal that deserved to succeed, and was likely to succeed, failed because the Russians took advantage of criticisms of the proposal in the Western press.

How pleasant and rewarding it is to look back and see how Walter Lippmann has kept all the balls in the air at once—loyalty to the West, understanding for America's allies, a sense of timing, and obedience to the compulsions of penetrating analysis and objective truth. He has not recorded only the stormy hours within the Western alliance. At every opportunity, he has put in a word for its strengthening and especially for the strengthening of Anglo-American understanding. When strains and differences have come, he has, almost always, been much severer on his own administration when saying who was to blame. It is, in fact, remarkable to recall how often, at times of differences between governments, a strong body of American opinion, including Walter Lippmann, and often led by him, has reached the same diagnosis as serious newspapers and independent-minded political representatives in Britain. This has formed a real bond in the alliance and has, I believe, often softened the intergovernmental disputes. Indeed, it can be argued that this common body of educated opinion is the real balancer, the governor, the regulator, of the alliance. Each government has to be aware of it in its action. Neither can go too long or too far against it.

Looking back, one can see how often it has played a healing part. Until the Suez affair, the lowest point in understanding between our two peoples came about the time of the large American loan in 1946, negotiated after the abrupt cessation of Lend-Lease. British people were painfully aware of how the war had impoverished them and drained their foreign holdings; many Americans all too clearly assumed that British troubles were made worse through inefficiency and socialism. But some of the grief and misunderstanding went as British writers pointed out that the loan was urgently necessary and American writers began to look ahead to something more imaginative and constructive. Ernest Bevin then took up the great work of building up the alliance and making the most of every American initiative. Within a few years, there came pressure on Britain, from some highly placed in Washington, to join in a West European federation. The warning came to "Federate—or else!" But, once again, there came the corrective from American writers who declared that so broad a federation was neither wise nor feasible. Since then, there has been, on the British side, the abiding sense of alliance, interrupted every so often, by a swing of opinion to one of two violent extremes. West European opinion has alternated even more violently. One day it is said that the United States would not, in the last resort, risk being involved in a nuclear war to defend a European ally. The next day has brought a louder cry that the United States is risking dragging us all into nuclear war by being too stubborn and threatening, especially in the Far East. Washington has every reason to be irritated beyond measure at such contradictory cries, but it can be said in all seriousness that British and Continental opinion would have swung still more violently, and the alarm would at times have been greater, except for one thing. That is our knowledge of the steady course being advocated throughout by a highly influential body of American opinion.

Those of us in Britain who, at the time of the Korean war, were writing that we saw nothing but folly and danger in General MacArthur's crossing of the famous parallel, and in his subsequent drive toward the Yalu, were fortified in our warnings when we found that Walter Lippmann and other Americans were uttering the same warnings. Later, during the Indochinese war, Walter Lippmann was much sharper than any British journalist, so far as I recall, against Mr. Dulles's and the Pentagon's apparent eagerness to intervene militarily when Dien-Bien-Phu was going or gone. Some of his words stuck in my mind, and I looked them up:

There is a notion in what might be described as highly irresponsible responsible quarters that, while it would be better to have allies than not to have them, it would be feasible for the United States alone to take over the war in Indo-China and win it. This is a most dangerous fantasy for men of power and influence to entertain.[2]

I remember talking to Sir Anthony Eden at Geneva at the time on his tussle with Mr. Dulles on this very matter. I know that he was relieved, and was convinced that the issue was not so critical and desperate, after he had read one or two of Walter Lippmann's articles, showing how strong was resistance inside America to any Indochina adventure. Later still, there came the two crises over the Chinese offshore islands, in 1955 and in 1958. Again there was the strong identity of view between many in Britain and the Americans that thought as Walter Lippmann did. Again, in a curious but marked way, this identity of view softened and largely prevented any dispute between the two nations as such. There could be no dispute on national lines when, from inside America, Walter Lippmann was writing that there could be a cease-fire if the Chinese Nationalists were pulled back to Formosa,[3] that the off-shore islands were a dangerous entanglement,[4] and that the policy toward China, founded on a lot of untruths, had led to the Chiang alliance, which was an enormous liability and "which, if it does not entangle us in war, is surely and steadily losing us the respect and confidence of our friends."[5]

No less remarkable and courageous was the scrupulous manner in which Walter Lippmann wrote when Britain

2 New York *Herald Tribune*, Paris edition, May 11, 1954.
3 New York *Herald Tribune*, Paris edition, April 15, 1955.
4 New York *Herald Tribune*, Paris edition, April 25, 1955.
5 New York *Herald Tribune*, Paris edition, September 12, 1958.

and France put themselves in the wrong over Suez. How many, indeed, were joining in the hue and cry, and how good it was—even for those British who were beside themselves with mortification at their government's act—to hear a steady and rational judgment. Walter Lippmann had been against any use of force. Yet when it came, he wrote that Britain and France had acted wrongly, but under great provocation,[6] and that the U.S. administration was wrong to go to the United Nations treating Israel as an aggressor while ignoring all the previous Egyptian raids.[7] "We should not allow ourselves to remain in the position, into which we have drifted and been pushed, where the whole weight of our influence is against the wrong done by our allies and no serious part of our influence is against the wrong done to our allies."[8] Only a man who had his eyes fixed on the main objective—the need to repair the alliance—could have written those cool and firm words at that emotional time.

This constant cross-fertilization of thought on so many subjects between British and Americans is, indeed, one of the fundamental facts of the alliance. Of course, each of us shares thoughts with groups in other allied countries and in many countries that are not allied. But in the Anglo-American exchanges, there is a special intellectual excitement, similar to exchanges within the Commonwealth, because there is the certain belief that the greater knowledge gained can have some effect on policy. At times, it has to be admitted, the most conspicuous effect has been negative—that is, in helping to stop one or another gov-

6 New York *Herald Tribune*, Paris edition, December 3, 1956.
7 New York *Herald Tribune*, Paris edition, November 5, 1956.
8 New York *Herald Tribune*, Paris edition, December 3, 1956.

ernment from going further on a rash and separate course. There has yet to be formulated a common school of thought on the Middle East or on Germany. The only certainty is that unless the two peoples are broadly agreed behind the two governments, the Western alliance can do nothing constructive. Certainly almost everyone in Britain would draw back from negotiations with Russia if we and the United States were seriously differing over Europe or over any major region of the world. In his own writings, Walter Lippmann has always borne the need for allied unity in mind and has often, I should say, curbed and disciplined his thoughts and suggestions to keep them within range of what he estimates to be—with a strong helping push—politically possible. An example of his awareness of the need for unity was shown in a change of emphasis in his articles as a result of a visit to Europe in late 1953. Earlier that year, even before Stalin's death, he had been hoping for negotiations for the withdrawal of troops from Germany, and had said that the Western powers had to prepare in their minds for a Europe in which Germany would be united and sovereign.[9] In October, writing from London, he was back on the need for allied unity, back, too, on hard facts, and he reported that no one (whether in Moscow, Bonn, Paris, or London) was ready to "live with a reunited and sovereign Germany."[10] Very soon he was saying that a German solution may take years to work out,[11] and in a remarkably prescient piece was advocating a simple *modus vivendi*, calling for a reduction of foreign troops, some disengagement, some slowing

[9] New York *Herald Tribune*, Paris edition, April 9, 1953.
[10] New York *Herald Tribune*, Paris edition, October 22, 1953.
[11] New York *Herald Tribune*, Paris edition, May 9, 1955.

down of German rearmament, and "various arrangements and accommodations between the two Germanys."[12] He was still tempted to go further, and before the end of 1955 he was saying that unless the West was ready to make Germany's membership in NATO negotiable (in order to get unification), "We must be prepared to see increasing intercourse and direct negotiation between the West and the East Germans."[13] In 1958, he was writing again that the the two Germanys would be brought into closer contact, and he was, indeed, wondering whether the West should not take up Mr. Khrushchev's offer of direct talks between the two Germanys.[14]

Other writers in this volume are, I fancy, going into the strategy of Walter Lippmann's ideas on Germany. Many people differ strongly from him. Leading articles in the London *Times* have taken a different line, emphasizing (long before Mr. Macmillan went off to Moscow) the need to begin with a controlled area of armaments and troops in Central Europe. That could be a start for relaxation. But, in dealing here mainly with the craftsmanship of his work—as a sustained intellectual exercise in analysis, argumentation, presentation, and timing—one can have nothing but the highest admiration. His dry, clear, Euclidian style of argument is admirably fashioned as a weapon of his mind. It can take account of political pressures and popular emotions without being deflected off course by them. He moves forward by logic, and at times, at the end of a piece, seems surprised at the conclusion to which logic has led him. (Perhaps Euclid was sometimes

[12] New York *Herald Tribune*, Paris edition, May 30, 1955.
[13] New York *Herald Tribune*, Paris edition, November 14, 1955.
[14] New York *Herald Tribune*, Paris edition, December 19, 1958.

surprised too.) This can cause him at times, as when discussing German reunification and the withdrawal of troops, to move on too fast too soon. But in the timing and presentation of his argument, he is scrupulously fair. He has cast much bread upon the waters. When thinking of how much has returned after many days, he can be sure, first and foremost, of the admiration of his colleagues in many lands. Who else, writing alone and under his own name, has kept up such a high level of hard thought and cogent proposals? He can be sure, too, that he has fostered the Anglo-American alliance in several direct ways. He has had a part, public and private, in shaping several of the great American decisions on the Marshall Plan and NATO. More than that, he has stimulated and enlarged that common body of thought and inquiry on great issues which is what I have called the regulator of the alliance. And he can be sure that his writings, read in so many countries, have given unnumbered people of influence a new and steadier view of the great world encounter. I remember his saying years ago that if he were convinced that a third world war was inevitable, he would give up writing. For every reason, we can be glad as we shake his hand now. He is still writing.

VIII

Interpreter of East and West

BY FRANK MORAES

Long before I met Walter Lippmann in India, I had been
familiar with his column, "Today and Tomorrow," and
had also read some of his books. The political columnist
was then a rarity in India, and has still to achieve the
status and popularity of his American counterpart. Visiting the United States during the last presidential election,
1956, I had occasion to meet Lippmann again and to discuss with him the prospects of Eisenhower and Stevenson.

Not all of his prognostications, as I recall them now,
were fulfilled, but his analysis of men and events was
unusual for its clarity and perceptiveness. These derived,
one felt, from his habit of assessing day-to-day happenings
against the broad sweep of the history of human progress
and thought. Lippmann is interesting on personalities, but
he thinks primarily in terms of principles.

This gives his column, as also his conversation, a curious
cerebral feel of scholarship and detachment, even if at
times the effortless omniscience of the pundit peeps
through. You might or might not agree with what he

writes or says. But he makes you think, probably because his comments on the day-to-day world are themselves the product of sustained uninterrupted thinking, not merely over days, but over years. Lippmann thinks and analyzes in terms of first principles. He also reaches his conclusions in the same context, which is why his long-range dissective processes are invariably sound while his judgments on ephemeral events are often unsure. Politics does not strike at the same pace or on the same plane as history.

Lippmann turns on politics the searchlight of philosophy and history. This approach is vividly demonstrated in his book *Essays in Public Philosophy*, published four years ago, wherein he denigrates the politician who leans on and is led by public opinion. "The decisive consideration [with the politician]," he observes, "is not whether the proposition is good but whether it is popular—not whether it will work well and prove itself but whether the active talking constituents like it immediately." In Lippmann's view, the principle of the natural law which sees politics in terms of philosophy and theology should be the basis of democracy and not the day-to-day fumblings of politicians with their eyes on the electorate.

Thus, as a political commentator, applying this yardstick to developing events, Lippmann writes of the world not as it will be, but as it should be. The intellectual honesty that characterizes his writing stems from this approach, and, along with his disinterestedness, it is his distinctive quality as a newspaperman. Twentieth-century diplomacy and politics, as he sees them, constitute a chain of tragic errors leading inevitably and inexorably to war. History repeats itself because men repeat their mistakes.

Conversely and correctly, Lippmann, as a journalist,

believes that his basic loyalty is to peoples and not to governments. Hence the epithets "neutralist" and "appeaser," which certain circles quite unjustly attach to him as a political label. Lippmann can never be a neutralist for the simple reason that his approach to politics is influenced by ethics and a sense of moral values, and because, moreover, he is enormously and actively interested in what happens and is going to happen to our world and to the peoples who inhabit it. His disinterestedness in parochial party politics does not imply indifference to national or international security and welfare, but a refusal—it may be, occasionally, Olympian—to pander to the pendulum passions.

It is this intellectual honesty and disinterested approach, combined with a basic concern for the people's good rather than for a government's survival or favor, which makes Lippmann a conspicuously respected political commentator in India. He has laid down standards, and observes them scrupulously. In India, as elsewhere, Lippmann's clientele is confined to the informed intelligentsia, since his writings presuppose more than an elementary knowledge of international affairs by the reader. This inevitably limits his following to a small but nonetheless influential number, and I have found that his name is known and highly regarded among many college students and the growing generation of our English-speaking youth.

The political columnist or commentator has still to come into his own in India, where the newspaper reader more often than not takes opinions from the editorials, which are perhaps more widely read and discussed in our country than in any other land. It does not follow from this that the average Indian reader's opinions are automatically molded by his newspaper, for most educated or even literate Indians tend to have definite political views, even if these are sharper and more defined at local or state levels than at the national level. But in India there is still a lack or dearth of the media or instruments of public opinion, such as radio and television commentators, independent newspapers, trade unions, and voluntary associations, which are to be found on a vastly more organized scale in the United States and many European countries.

Even where these media operate in our country, they are restricted for the most part to the urban intelligentsia, who form a microscopic proportion of the population. India's literacy rate is a little over 20 per cent. But the Indian is naturally articulate and curious, and knowledge, along with opinions and information, has a habit of percolating to wide masses of the people. While Europe's civilizations grew largely in cities such as Athens, Rome, and Florence, the civilizations of Asia, especially in India and Southeast Asia, emerged from the villages. Thus, the villages remain receptive to ideas from the urban areas, where the old traditional structure is breaking down and where traditional values are being disrupted. I mention this parenthetically because the impact of even foreign ideas is more widely pervasive in India than is imagined abroad.

In stating this, I do not mean to suggest that Lippmann's name is known in our villages. However, the ideas he represents are ideas that have a close affinity to the thought pattern of the average educated Indian, particularly in the field of international policy and relations, and it is through the educated Indian that the illiterate peasant and villager in rural India largely derive their own ideas. The Indian peasant may not have heard of Czechoslovakia, but if he is told of two great power blocs contending for the soul of the world, his natural reaction would instinctively be to keep out of both. This is where Lippmann's thinking rings a bell in most Indian minds. "The world," he has written, "will have to be big enough to let differing systems of life and of government exist side by side." What else is this but the principle of "peaceful coexistence"?

I myself do not subscribe wholeheartedly to this creed, since I believe that Communism by its very nature cannot cease to be expansionist. It might temporarily call a halt or even reverse in its tracks, but sooner or later the Red steam-roller moves remorselessly ahead. Yet in India, as in the developing countries of Asia, where political freedom is meaningless without economic independence, a peaceful breathing space is a major imperative, and the more protracted the better.

With India, Lippmann also feels that Red China should have a seat in the United Nations, though he has, of course, arrived at this conclusion through his own cerebral processes, uninfluenced by New Delhi. In certain respects, he goes beyond Delhi's official thinking. He has endorsed, for instance, the idea of "confederation" of East and West Germany and supported the withdrawal of Western and Russian occupation troops, leaving the two neutralized Germanys to work out their own destiny, a solution which has been close to that of the Kremlin.

Here is the intellectual isolationist as opposed to the political neutralist at work, a man subsisting solely in the ivory tower of his own thinking but moved basically more by human needs and considerations than by political motivations. Lippmann's experience is grounded in politics, practical and academic, and his range in both fields is considerable and impressive. It is perhaps not without significance that in World War I he served as an intelligence agent in France and as the interpreter of President Wilson's Fourteen Points, while, significantly also, he worked in his youth as an assistant to a philosopher and a politician, to George Santayana and Woodrow Wilson. In Lippmann's mental make-up there survive the intelligence agent, the idealist, the philosopher, and the politician. But the humanist predominates.

There Lippmann is curiously near Gandhi, who also had these components in his personality, though the two men are temperamentally and in other respects widely disparate and apart. Gandhi, like Lippmann more a humanist than a politician, was inclined to reach out for what *should* be rather than for what *would* be. He put human values above political necessities and could keep the entire Congress Working Committee waiting while he patiently listened to an aged widow's tale of woe. "Who can say?" a spectator of that scene remarked to me later. "His sense of values might be more true than ours."

Like Gandhi, Lippmann is more interested in the purpose than in the mechanics of politics, but, while taking a long-range view of human and political history, he is, unlike Gandhi, not a pragmatist in his methods. "One step enough for me" was the Mahatma's credo. I remember asking Nehru not long ago why it was that while Gandhi attacked untouchability, he supported caste.

"I asked him that question myself," Nehru recalled. "In fact, I had a long discussion with him. He listened to me very patiently and at the end disarmed me with one question: 'Don't you realize, Jawahar, that if untouchability goes, caste goes? Why do you want to stir a hornet's nest?' "

That is precisely what India's Prime Minister revels in doing. Many years ago, at the height of the Congress controversy with the Muslim League, Nehru remarked with a show of willfulness: "Mr. Jinnah complains that I am out to create new situations. I *am* out to create new situations."

Lippmann, far from attempting to create new situations, would like to resolve old ones, but he approximates to Nehru insofar as both men, while willing to peep, even peer, into the future, are both eager to define ultimate objectives, whether political, economic, or social. Nehru, being a socialist with pronounced Marxist leanings, has his own definite ideas of a Socialist paradise on earth, or at least in India, whereas Lippmann, who might be described as a Wilsonian liberal internationally and a Rooseveltian liberal at home, has, in all likelihood, ultimate political and economic concepts far removed from Nehru's. Yet both men like to view the world through wide-open windows looking out to far-away horizons.

This dual affinity of Lippman's with Gandhi and Nehru struck me forcefully during a conversation with him at the Metropolitan Club in Washington shortly before the last presidential election. He spoke warmly of Eisenhower except on one point, where he compared him with Roosevelt to Eisenhower's disadvantage.

"Roosevelt had no respect for the rich," Lippmann remarked. "Eisenhower has. He is not politically shrewd. He believes that people who can amass money are necessarily talented."

It was a point, I reflected, which Nehru would have relished, though he, like Lippmann, knew affluence.

Lippmann went on to make another observation, which would have had Gandhi's approval but not Nehru's.

"If Stevenson wins," he said, although he did not rate his chances high, "the Democrats will go left of center and so might the Republicans. That wouldn't be good for America, which should always keep to the middle of the road."

It was a typical Gandhian approach, the attitude of offending neither the right nor the left while pursuing your own path. But it did not square entirely with America's international policy, though doubtless Lippmann was referring only to the national situation. That is where Nehru, whose economic policy at home is left of center, would not have reacted kindly.

Lippmann's humanistic approach to political problems and his genuine zeal to see things clearly and to see them whole make him an ideal interpreter between the advanced countries on both sides of the Atlantic and the developing countries of Asia, Africa, and Southeast Asia. He has no ax to grind, political, economic, or social. It is not because his mind is in a state of constant flux or his ideas are inchoate, but because he prefers to rely on the ultimate ascendancy of human reason and on the triumph of common sense and good will. He prefers, as he himself has put it, to stand apart from the crowd and to fix his eyes "on a longer past and a longer future" than those perturbed with recurring crises and anxious about what tomorrow holds. Lippmann's ultimate faith is in man and humanity, irrespective of color, creed, or conviction. His is pre-eminently a civilized mind and voice. He is often caught in the tension between his belief in man and reason and his realization that man often ignores reason and is led to tragic error.

Of course, he has made mistakes both in interpretation

and judgment. He may be less fallible than most, but he has claimed no infallibility for himself. Some accuse him of posturing as a high pontiff in too many sanctuaries— a charge, like that of inconsistency, that any man who exposes his views and judgments to the public gaze continuously over the years lays himself open to. It cannot be said that other people's opinions on his work disturb Lippmann unduly. But I think that such imperviousness does not arise from intellectual arrogance or conceit, but from an inner certitude of mind and spirit about the bigger things that matter.

What are these? So far as India is concerned, a similar certitude of mind and spirit that, in her struggle toward economic independence, the West, more particularly the United States and Britain, will not hesitate to help India to achieve that goal more rapidly than any other country in Asia. Japan achieved it through her Meiji revolution, though conditions, political and economic, have changed greatly since then and might alter even more rapidly during the next decade. But time is against India and the West.

I can frankly think of few American journalists who could advocate such assistance more convincingly than Lippmann, for during the last war he took an attitude toward the Congress party almost as critical as the then British raj might have liked it. India at the time did not relish his approach to the problem of democracy and colonial oppression, though the hindsight of history might possibly in the long run prove him right, for here again was another Lippmann demonstration of fixing one's eyes "on a longer past and a longer future." In this case, events have proved Lippmann's assessment and verdict right.

Asia, particularly India, thinks of him today as an unusual American commentator, able to fix and interpret
events in the proper perspective of history. This is because
the Orient is convinced of his fair-mindedness, of his
ability to assess, praise, and criticize peoples and governments irrespective of whether their political or international alignments at any given period coincide or are opposed to the outlook and policies of his own government.
In that sense, Lippmann is the only true internationalist
who in the general madness of the postwar period has kept
his head, refusing to be deflected from the principles which
to many of his critics appeared to be flatulent platitudes
outdated by time.

It is not that, like Peter Pan, Lippmann has refused to
grow up. I think that it is we who have often criticized
him, and have even questioned his motives, who have
stubbornly declined to see developments in a perspective
that deludes us, who have made it difficult to stretch our
hands across the vast gulf that separates the democracies
from the totalitarian states which now stare stonily at us.

Although I have often disagreed with what I have read
in Lippmann's "Today and Tomorrow" columns, I must
confess that he has been more often right on tomorrow
than I have been on today—even in matters affecting Asia
and my own country. More than anything else, it is the
monumental patience and persistence of political prophets
and analysts such as Lippmann which testify to the real
strength of democracy—the faith that might err along the
by-lanes but will never falter on the broad highways of
history, that sees the vision big and feels, despite dis-
couragement and revilement, that it can make it great.

Lippmann is a prophet who, despite being confounded

in his own time, holds a superlative place among the fear-
lessly honest political prognosticators of his day. And that
day has been cloudy, confused, and contradictory for all.
Why does Asia, particularly India, trust him? Because he
is a man who can be trusted, who invites trust and respects
it. In Asia, nobody has the heart or callousness to break
his neighbor's begging bowl. Yet in the West, including
the United States, more generous than most, there have
been many who over months of crisis and famine have
dangled food as a political bait before the starving, hungry,
and unoffending millions who constitute Asia's masses.

Somerset Maugham, describing his own craftsmanship,
once said that he liked to get down to the bare bones of
style. One might observe of Walter Lippmann that he has
always attempted to get down to the heart of the matter,
to see through the cold eye of his political microscope the
feverish minds, the desperate hearts, and the empty stomachs of many millions of his fellow-men, striving like him
to reach out to a new world, not perhaps of mental endeavor, but of material achievement, which, whatever the
moralists, European and Asian, might say, is the one spring-
board to moral fulfillment. He has realized what many
allegedly acute Western observers have still to appreciate
—that hungry men think through their stomachs rather
than through their minds.

And so, on his seventieth birthday, I should like to
salute him as a prophet who, though often proved wrong
in his lifetime and in his country, still retains the respect
of all who admire courage—in many ways the more difficult kind of courage, moral courage, being unafraid to
write or speak the truth as he sees it because tomorrow
will confound what he says today. The one reason why I

think and feel that Walter Lippmann in his personality and writings represents the truly global or international man of today is because, like Gandhi, he sees history as a flowing stream blending the past, present, and future in a continuous pattern, sometimes broken but always finally blended, the one leading to the other in an eventually multi-colored, harmonious, many-faceted sequence. That will happen when One World is achieved—the dream of the civilized men and women of today.

IX

Apostle of Excellence: The View from Afar

BY HARRY S. ASHMORE

When I entered upon the practice of journalism almost a quarter-century ago, Walter Lippmann had already attained the settled status of a public monument. In normal course, a young reporter could expect to encounter the other household names of his trade; if he were lucky, on some memorable evening after the night leads had been filed, he might wind up in a corner booth with such an ambulant legend as H. L. Mencken. But Lippmann was seen, if at all, only across the great spiritual void that separates the press bench from the head table.

In my time, Lippmann has not even shown up at the national political conventions, which are also great journalistic reunions where the more austere editors and their publishers wear working-press credentials with almost unseemly pride, and commonly repair to the clamorous press pens to savor rumors that are, if no more reliable than those current on the floor, somewhat better told. I understand, however, that since the advent of the electronic age, Lippmann has made an important concession; during these quadrennial climaxes of political fever, he abandons his hot-weather retreat in Maine and returns to Washington, where the television reception is better.

The picture of a solitary Lippmann gazing into a television tube darkly, hundreds of miles from the hall where the news has its focus, does no violence to the image he has projected to his readers over the years. It is the conceit of most commentators that they are really reporters—reporters of a superior sort, to be sure, and willing to venture an opinion based on erudition as well as personal observation, but still legmen at heart, responding to the alarms of history with the alacrity they once accorded the bells that rang in the city hall press rooms of their youth. Douglass Cater has noted that this addiction to the humble title is particularly pronounced among the Washington coterie. "The Washington correspondent," he has written, "clings to the image of the reporter as the supreme individual in the age of the organization man." The elegant brothers Alsop once said of their mission: "Above all reporting offers the sense of being *engagé* in the political process of one's own time." Lippmann, who began his journalistic career at the top, presumably has never followed a fire truck in his life, and certainly has given no indication that he ever had the impulse to do so. He offers not engagement, but massive detachment.

This alone makes Lippmann unique in a calling whose practitioners range from the common gossip to the common scold, and are united only by a common endeavor to leave the impression that they have access to the world's privy councils. He is not the only columnist who hands down his opinions ex cathedra, but he is the only one who deliberately writes as though he derives his authority solely from a relentless study of the public record; it is much easier to visualize Lippmann reaching for a file folder than for a telephone. A constant reader will assume that the author is on familiar terms with the world's statesmen, or at least those of the rank of prime minister and above, but this is an effect achieved without name-dropping, personal anecdote, or reminiscence. Indeed, the assumption includes a feeling that these people come to see Lippmann, not he them. The imagination balks at the thought of Lippmann currying favor with a congressman in order to unplug a pipeline.

Lippmann is not a reporter, then, and makes no pretense of being one, and there is even reason to doubt that in his own mind he identifies himself within the loose limits of the generic term "newspaperman." Early in his career he wrote: "If we assume . . . that news and truth are two words for the same thing, we shall, I believe, arrive nowhere." The best that news can do, in his view, is "signalize an event," while the function of truth is "to bring to light the hidden facts, to set them into relation with each other, and to make a picture of reality on which men can act." Elaborating upon this thesis many years later in discussion with a group of Nieman Fellows, he said that he conceived of his column as an effort to keep contemporary events in such perspective that his readers would have no reason to be surprised when something of importance occurred. As the standing title of his essays, "Today and Tomorrow," suggests, Lippmann operates on the premise that a man who understands the past and views the present without passion ought to be able to call the turn on the future.

This concept has produced a style of writing admirably adapted to it; one has the feeling that Lippmann's precise words were selected to be graven in stone rather than committed to soft and transient newsprint. For this reason, and because Lippmann writes primarily of ideas and only incidentally of men, it is commonly believed that he is hard to read. This is true only in the sense that he deals with hard and frequently unpleasant truths, which in themselves demand a certain flexing of the intellectual muscles. Actually, his prose style is a model of lucidity, so much so that it is almost impossible for the least scholarly reader to misunderstand his meaning. The best evidence of this may lie in the fact that no one has ever successfully satirized Lippmann, even though he operates in a medium where the faint aura of pomposity inherent in his stance constitutes a standing invitation to burlesque.

Whether Lippmann's aloof and almost bloodless public manner is an accurate reflection of the inner man, or a shield behind which he protects his privacy, is a matter of speculation in which I am not competent to engage. But certainly it is an essential instrument in the execution of the role he has chosen for himself. His style is that of a man who operates at considerable remove from those who occupy the center of the stage of history. Thus, he appears as an informed observer without personal commitment to any individual, or even to any fixed point of view, and is absolved of the suspicion that he might use his considerable powers to reward a friend or punish an enemy. The impression, whether it is accurate or not, is that in his long passage through high places he has remained singularly free of the human obligations that accrete to lesser men and sometimes blur their view.

This image is deliberately cultivated and jealously guarded. The slightest degree of personal interest in the matter at hand, and therefore of possible bias, is meticulously noted—as in Lippmann's first comment after the United States Supreme Court decision on school segregation in 1954. After reviewing the development of the constitutional issue from the adoption of the Fourteenth Amendment in 1868, he characteristically dismissed the optimistic statements of official Washington with a warning that the nation "can afford to have no illusion about the magnitude of the efforts which will be needed to apply the ruling efficiently and successfully." At the midpoint of this disquisition, he dropped in a pair of parentheses and inserted this note: "The facts about this [the dual school system] and a background of the whole problem can be found in a report by Harry S. Ashmore on 'The Negro and the Schools.'. . . This study and the report were financed by the Fund for the Advancement of Education, which is a subsidiary of the Ford Foundation. I should say for the sake of the record that I am a member of the Board of the Fund. . . ." And so he was, although this was a fact of which I was aware only from reading the flyleaf of the Fund's annual report; he had never at any time communicated with me or in any fashion attempted to influence the direction of the study.

One important result of this calculated disengagement is that Lippmann, although he has expressed firm, forthright, and often unpopular opinions on every important public issue for almost half a century, is not, in the current usage, a controversial figure. He may occasionally stir some passion in upper intellectual reaches, but this is never translated into the kind of public outcry that is likely to send a circulation manager into emergency consultation with his publisher. One reason, doubtless, is that in his careful weighing and balancing of the factors that shape great issues he is rarely entirely satisfactory to the partisans on either side. This is so in the current, highly emotional controversy over segregation—the domestic problem which, with its constitutional overtones, occupies as much of his attention as any other.

Lippmann accepts the Supreme Court rulings in the school cases as morally and legally correct. But at the same time, he contends that, as a practical matter, segregation cannot be ended immediately in the Southern states without placing an undue and dangerous strain upon the federal system and the judicial process—typically giving a higher priority to this aspect of the matter than to the demands of the Negro minority for social justice. There is no comfort here for the National Association for the Advancement of Colored People, or for the white Citizens Councils, and very little for the disconsolate majority caught between the polar opinions of the action groups. I would agree that Lippmann has here successfully pursued truth according to his formula, and has made a picture of reality upon which men can act. But it is not a picture that is likely to be acceptable to Federal Judge George Bell Timmerman of South Carolina, who not long ago described his position thus, "He that is not with me is against me; and he that gathereth not with me scattereth abroad"—a sentiment ascribed to Jesus Christ but also doubtless wholly acceptable to Roy Wilkins as a statement of policy.

Still, Lippmann endures on Southern editorial pages and is not much castigated. He is no part of a Southern hero, as is his contemporary David Lawrence, who evokes a mighty chorus of rebel yells with his constant flagellation of the Supreme Court. But neither has Lippmann become a pariah for voicing the essentially moderate view that has placed some Southern editors and politicians beyond the pale. Even in a season of unrestrained rhetoric, Lippmann maintains an impervious respectability.

It is this, I suspect, more than any other factor that gained for Lippmann the widest syndication ever accorded a serious newspaper column, and maintained for him most of his major outlets across the nation as he cut back his output to two a week. His column undoubtedly has been purchased on occasion largely for prestige, but never for balance—as was often the case with the late Thomas Stokes, an unreconstructed New Dealer who derived considerable pleasure from the fact that, as a minor token of free expression, he appeared across the page from some of the most reactionary editorial columns in the country. It is, in fact, almost impossible to place Lippmann in the political spectrum in accordance with any of the usual litmus tests currently in use: he will show liberal on one issue and conservative on another, and the passing of time has often changed the hue while his own position remained constant.

Assembling the facts so that other men may act upon them is, of course, an act of advocacy in its own right—although it might be contended that all Lippmann really advocates is general enlightenment rather than material progress in the standard American pattern, which he is likely to view with suspicion. Because he flies no factional banner, his astringent judgments have a special impact. I doubt that any of the commentators who have had great sport with President Eisenhower's penchant for golf, Western stories, Chamber of Commerce cronies, and garbled syntax have ever written a more devastating paragraph than the one that concluded Lippmann's memorable 1957 column on the advent of sputnik:

With prosperity acting as a narcotic, with Philistinism and McCarthyism rampant, our public life has been increasingly doped and without purpose. With the president in a kind of partial retirement, there is no standard raised to which the people can repair. Thus we drift with no one to state our purposes and to make policy, into a chronic disaster like Little Rock. We find ourselves then without a chart in very troubled waters.

Even here, however, it will be noted that Lippmann is impeccably impersonal; his criticism is of the partial vacancy of the presidential office, not of its part-time occupant, and his concern is with the effect this has had upon the delicate instrumentality of popular government, in which he maintains an almost proprietary interest.

I have seen an adverse opinion from Lippmann spread sadness and even despair in high political circles, but rarely anger. Under these circumstances, the most volatile politician is more likely to be moved to a somber examination of his own conscience than to seize a horsewhip and call out his detractor. This, I suppose, is because Lippmann's voice comes from above and not from below; it certainly could not be confused with the voice of the people, which is the politician's most immediate concern, but it commands attention nevertheless. It may not be correct to assume that on all or even on most occasions Lippmann is the tribune of the national community of thinking men, but it is never safe to assume that he isn't.

It is possible to measure the circulation of Lippmann's journalistic writing, but there is no reliable guide to the actual readership. The polls by which newspapers test the popularity of their features could easily go astray in this instance; I suspect that the country is full of people who would, in the same way they find it necessary to profess familiarity with Shakespeare, say that they read Lippmann when in fact they do not. The size of his audience, however, is not so important as its quality, which is unquestionably high. It may be assumed that Lippmann's regular readers include most of those who currently are called "eggheads" and discounted in practical matters, but among them there is also a substantial number of men of affairs and influence scattered through most of our cities, large and small. My estimate would be that he still speaks of the higher things to more of these than any other journalist now practicing.

The traveler may find new appreciation of Lippmann's special meaning and unique status when he journeys into one of the great American journalistic deserts. (Texas and California spring to mind.) Here he will find a preponderance of newspapers that limit their editorial discussion of international affairs to an occasional chauvinistic bellow, and of national issues to a restatement of local prejudices; the voyager may even get the desperate feeling that he won't hear of anything that happens east of the Rockies or north of Red River unless he gets a letter from home.

Here "Today and Tomorrow" is an oasis; Lippmann's cool judgments, restrained prophecies and long view remind that the great world is still there—tortured, divided, wracked by crisis, but under the watchful eye of one who understands it.

In varying degree, this condition is now visible everywhere in the country, and is becoming more so as newspapers become fewer and increasingly beset by the notion that their survival depends upon entertaining their readers. Promotion managers are on the ascendant; editorial writers are enjoined to write shorter sentences rather than to think higher thoughts; newsprint is too precious to waste on anything that won't be read by everybody; year by year, television takes a larger bite of the advertising dollar; and the publisher of the San Francisco *Chronicle* has proudly explained the discovery that enabled him to resuscitate that ailing journal: "International news is not what people want to read at breakfast." In this *milieu*, the suspicion arises that Lippmann is not unique solely because he is inimitable; he also may stand out as did the last mastodon to survive the changing environment.

In the ultimate appraisal, it may turn out that Lippmann's undoubted influence on his time has been negative. It is no more possible to imagine his readers rising up in concerted purpose to carry a national election than it is to imagine his joining the shakers and movers. On the other hand, he has consistently led a substantial and important group of Americans in the kind of intellectual setting-up exercises that increase the sensibilities and guard against the human tendency to turn down a blind alley in search of the quick-and-easy answer. He has regularly served up food for thought in unlikely places where precious little was otherwise available. Above all, he has been an apostle of excellence in an era of the common denominator—and it is, I think, a matter of more than my own professional concern that his tribe is decreasing.

X

The Democratic Elite and American Foreign Policy

BY REINHOLD NIEBUHR

The hazards of foreign policy in a democracy are well known. Contrary to the expectations of such eighteenth-century idealists as our own Thomas Jefferson and William Godwin of England, for instance, who hoped that democratic nations would eliminate all the problems of foreign policy, which they ascribed to the greed and malice of the kings and rulers, foreign policy has proved to be the Achilles heel of democracy. The obvious reason is that the average voter has only enough wisdom and knowledge to judge the policies of government when they impinge directly upon his life, but without aid he cannot come to an adequate judgment when the government affects the life of other nations. He knows only when the shoe pinches his own foot, though even in this case, he may not know the reasons for the cobbler's errors.

In foreign policy, democracy has one clear advantage over despotism or traditional monarchies. This advantage is derived from the reluctance of the common man to engage in hazardous martial ventures. His governments are bound to heed this reluctance, and, consequently, democracies, unlike dictatorships, are not inclined to engage in capricious or dangerous ventures in the relations with other nations. But even this advantage implies the weakness that democracies frequently cannot risk war when such a risk must be taken. An additional weakness of democratic foreign policy is that the passions which are aroused, and must be aroused to nerve the people for the sacrifice of war, tend to produce a vindictiveness, which makes a stable or decent peace impossible. Furthermore, the general public is not inclined to countenance the necessary sacrifices for preserving the posture of strength after the victorious war, so that democratic armies are frequently dispersed too quickly. The "Khaki election" in Britain, with its slogan "Hang the Kaiser and make the Germans pay" after World War I, is a vivid example of the first weakness; and our too-rapid dispersal of the armies that defeated Nazi Germany, leaving the field to the ally of yesterday and foe of today, Russia, is an example of the second weakness. Walter Lippmann, in his volume *Essays in Public Philosophy*, has given a vivid analysis of the weaknesses of democratic foreign policy, which remains persuasive, even if one does not share confidence in his cure for this weakness. That cure is a strong executive. This answer to the problem is not convincing because the United States has a stronger executive than any other democracy; but the President is finally responsible and responsive to public opinion, and must be, if a free society is to be maintained. There is, in short, no substitute for embarking upon every venture of education, in both the academic and journalistic realms of education, designed to make public opinion adequate to the responsibilities that it must bear in a democratic society.

I find myself in a quandary in regard to Lippmann's conception of the "public philosophy." The quandary is created by the fact that I heartily agree with everything he has written journalistically and in his occasional writings in an effort to alter the inadequacies of our "public philosophy." In these, he seems to me to offer valuable correctives for our political orientation. Yet I am not convinced by the argument of the impressive volume that bears the title *The Public Philosophy*. For in that volume he has a political and a moral answer for the predicament of modern democracy as it faces foreign policy problems neither of which seems to me to be convincing.

His political answer is the establishment of a stronger executive power. This is not convincing for reasons previously stated. If our executive power were stronger than it now is, it would become irresponsible (or partly irresponsible, as the power of the president in the Fifth Republic of France now is).

His moral answer is the restitution of "natural-law" norms. Traditional conceptions of natural law presuppose a classical ontology, which equates history with nature and does not allow for the endless contingencies of history and the variety of its configurations. If we do full justice to these contingencies, our norms are bound to be no more precise than the general feeling that there are standards of justice which transcend any conceivable positive law.

The responsibilities of a democratic society have been increased tremendously in recent decades. They have increased in our own nation for the obvious reason that we exercise great power in the alliance of noncommunist nations. We are, in fact, the hegemonous nation in this alliance; and we have had the responsibilities of this power thrust upon us with only the briefest apprenticeship in the arts of foreign policy. Until the beginning of World War I, our infancy was rocked in the cradle of seeming continental security, and we did not even know, as Lippmann observed, that this security was parasitic on the power of the British Navy. The responsibilities of great power have made the isolationism of the nineteenth century a thing of the past, but the present weight of power and responsibility has not endowed us automatically with commensurate wisdom.

In addition to the particular additional hazards which our democratic nation faces by reason of our peculiar history, with its great jump from comparative weakness to seeming omnipotence, we share with other democratic nations new complexities and perplexities in foreign policy, which are briefly defined as a "cold war" with the communist bloc of nations under Russian hegemony, the perils of nuclear annihilation, should this tension get out of hand, and the ever-growing complexity of the nuclear arsenal of weapons and missiles.

Any democratic nation, if it is not to abdicate foreign policy to an elite of experts, must be assiduous in expanding both its knowledge and its wisdom in regard to the issues and the facts which are the raw stuff of foreign policy. This "raw stuff" of foreign policy might be divided into three categories. 1) A reassessment of the political philosophy that informs our posture in the world. This re-examination is important particularly for us because the political philosophy that informs the public conscience is derived from a system of democratic idealism, conceived in the eighteenth century and defective in a realistic estimate of the factors of power and interest in the political sphere in general and in foreign policy in particular.

2) The best possible and most comprehensive knowledge of the world upon which our power impinges. Included in this world are the democratic nations, who are in various states of intimate alliance with us, the new nations of Asia and Africa, who are informed by various degrees of residual resentment against the past imperial dominance over them of the Western nations, and in various degrees of political and economic growing pains because of the novelty of their political autonomy and the friction between the new technical civilization into which they have been initiated and the agrarian or pastoral economies of their recent past. This world also includes our real or potential enemies of the "communist camp," comprising both Russia and China, the European satellites, and the various African and Asian nations that have fallen under communist dominance.

3) The raw stuff of an adequate foreign policy consists finally of as much comprehension as it is possible for laymen to absorb about the technics of modern warfare. One of the hazards of the present situation is that the technical decisions are more and more withdrawn from popular scrutiny, not only before information about them is "classified," that is, secret, but because, even if published, the general public has difficulty in mastering the technical details sufficiently to make significant and wise judgments on issues in which technical details impinge upon ultimate issues, whether, for instance, it is necessary to preserve equality of nuclear power if war is to be

avoided; and, if equality is necessary, whether it must be absolute equality in every department of the fearful modern nuclear arsenal; and whether equality in conventional as well as nuclear weapons is necessary. It is patently not possible for the general public to master all the technical details which belong to the raw stuff of foreign policy; but it is not possible either for the general public to master all the knowledge of both our friends and our foes that an adequate policy requires, or, for that matter to think through the problems of a political philosophy which must furnish the frame of meaning in which all the particular facts and issues must be organized.

Any realistic analysis of what is required for an adequate foreign policy must lead to the question about the relation of an aristocracy of informed men and women to the general electorate. Obviously the total public has neither the ability nor the inclination to master all the details required for an adequate policy. Democracy requires an aristocracy for an adequate foreign policy as it requires an aristocracy of knowledgeable and wise leaders in every realm of policy. The real question is: What kind of an aristocracy? Certainly not a tight or self-appointed aristocracy, nor a hereditary one. The health of a democracy requires a fluid and, if possible, multiple aristocracy, consisting of classes and of media of education in the community who select themselves and are selected by their interest in and ability to understand the many facets of foreign policy. Perhaps "aristocracy" is the wrong word for designating a selected group or groups in a community which have competence above the average public. Ideally, a free society creates various aristocracies or elite groups in various fields of culture and political affairs. In public affairs, the elected officials of government form a natural political aristocracy; but a democracy requires an additional aristocracy of informed and knowledgeable men in the electorate, who are able to judge the performance of their elected officials.

The most obvious second category of aristocracy in public affairs in a democracy consists of the educators, who supply the historical perspective and the technical competence for adequate judgments in these affairs. We have tentatively divided the educators into two classes, the "academic" and the "journalistic" educators. But this division must not be regarded as too fixed. Good journalistic commentators and "columnists" of Walter Lippmann's type not only reach wider audiences but they deal more profoundly with the issues of the day than many academic schoolmen. It is necessary to keep our conception of aristocracy fluid in every category. In every category the elite is chosen and chooses itself by its competence in serving the general public by its performance in making knowledge and skill available for the adequate judgment of public affairs.

The third category of the elite is even more vague and multiple than the first and second categories. It consists of those members of the general public who have, either by special training or special interest and capacity, become competent in public, particularly in foreign, affairs. This category of the elite certainly is not limited to citizens with college degrees. They may have other sources of insight than those supplied by good history and political-science courses. They may be devoted readers of one of the wise columnists, or of a newspaper that gives more than

ordinary attention to foreign affairs; or they may have
sources of insight derived from their ordinary vocation and
not from any of their educators. In the great debate before
World War II, in which the nation had the task of growing out of its isolationist illusions and recognizing both the
extent of its new power and the responsibilities that were
the concomitants of that power, two rather disparate classes
were members of the elite in foreign affairs, proved so by
the competence of their judgments. I refer to the taxi
drivers and the "international bankers." Both classes were
free of the liberalistic and moralistic illusions that infected
the clerical and academic elite of church and university
and gave a pacifist taint to the political judgments of the
nation. The taxi drivers, who certainly belonged to the
"lesser breed without the law," from the perspective of
the academic community, had their insight by virtue of a
native common sense and earthly wisdom, which arrived
at conclusions by effecting direct analogies between human
problems within their experience and the collective problems of mankind.

The international bankers, who were "beyond the pale,"
in the ideology of the left, which had been indirectly
influenced by Marxist propaganda, had an understanding
derived from their world-wide connections. Their understanding of America's role in world affairs was not significantly blurred by the admixture of economic interest
which entered into their calculations. At any rate, we must
not expect absolutely untainted or disinterested wisdom
in public affairs. Anyone approximating Plato's "philosopher king," who completely transcends the competition
of interests in the community, has long since been rele-
gated to the realm of utopia. And open society winnows

truth from error partly by allowing a free competition of interests and partly by establishing a free market of competing ideas.

One more category of the elite must be trained with reference to our foreign responsibilities. This comprises all the specialists who must act as the agents of American power and responsibility in every part of the world in which our power impinges and our responsibilities are exercised.

These specialists are naturally trained in our academic institutions and in such quasi-academic institutions as the War College, which fortunately withdraws some of the more promising junior officers of the various military and foreign services from their immediate duties to give them further training. But the foundation for the training of American proconsuls must be laid in our ordinary academic institutions. It is necessary to realize the paramount importance of training this group of specialists because there is no tradition in America which would dispose young men to prepare themselves for foreign service and there is no general recognition of the fact that we have in fact become a nation wielding imperial power and must have trained proconsuls for our imperium. The Russians are outstripping us in this type of training, though they are equally new in their imperial responsibilities. Perhaps it is not irrelevant to observe that the study of foreign languages, in which our high schools are particularly defective, is a necessary prerequisite for such foreign-service training. Our foreign representatives require more than foreign languages. They must be conversant with the problems faced by all the new nations as they move from a pastoral or agrarian economy to the complexities of a technical or industrial civilization, which destroys the old organic forms of community. The slogan of "raising living standards" is not enough as a source of wisdom for our representatives. It makes the important economic component in the life of the new nations into the sole objective. But the problem in all the new nations is how to relate technical competence to the resources of their old history that make for political stability and communal unity.

Nor is it enough that our representatives use the slogans of anti-imperialism, inherited from our revolutionary past, expecting it to be an open-sesame to the hearts of the new nations. We cannot, as one British journalist observed, be at the same time "The pillar of society and the vanguard of the revolution." We cannot aspire to be a member of the Bandung Conference of colored or Asian and African nations.

It is true that we were not involved in the imperial ventures that dominated the relations of the European nations and the technically underdeveloped nations of Asia and Africa in the nineteenth century, except for our brief excursion into overt imperialism after the Spanish-American War. But this does not change the fact that we are now the most powerful nation among the Western democracies, and that our hegemony must be exercised in a situation in which communist propaganda makes indiscriminate charges against Western "imperialism" and its supposed intimate relation with capitalism.

The situation in which we are called to exercise hegemonous power is further complicated by the great success of Britain, the "imperial" nation of the nineteenth century par excellence, in liquidating her empire or transmuting it into a commonwealth of nations; and by the comparative failure of France to transmute the French empire into a viable French Union. We may well believe that the French failure aids and abets the communist cause, but we must preserve an open mind toward the efforts of the Fifth Republic under De Gaulle to transmute the French Empire into a "French Community." The Fifth Republic seems bound to fail in Algeria, dogged as it is by a curious combination of imperial and liberal illusions. But it may yet be creative in black Africa. Our partnership with France is, at any rate, a necessity for the survival of the alliance of free nations.

Perhaps the greatest need is that an elite of the general public be encouraged and helped to rethink the political philosophy, or at least the political and moral presuppositions that govern the attitudes of the nation in the conduct of foreign policy. For such a reorientation, the services of educational leaders, both academic and journalistic, are required. We have previously observed that thoughtful columnists who deal not only with events of the day, but with the outlook of the nation in coming to terms with these events make the distinction between journalism and the university vague and indistinct. Those who benefit from their guidance are also a not too distinct group of the electorate who may or may not have the benefit of a "higher education."

The public philosophy of the nation is defective on various counts. The most obvious defect is that it does not seriously come to terms with the realities of power and interest in the world of nations. It does not recognize, for instance, the obvious fact that nations are "moral" in the sense of concerning themselves with interests other than their own only insofar as these interests concur with the nation's own interests. Failure to recognize this universal characteristic of the morality of nations, determined by the power and persistence of collective self-regard, gives the national attitude an air of self-righteous complacency, which our friends as well as our foes find vexatious, though our foes have their own, and possibly more grievous, sources of self-righteous complacency, for they are informed by a utopian creed, according to which the only "righteous" nations are those who have rid themselves of the institution of property in a revolution.

The blandness of our complacency is aggravated by the fact that political leaders consistently assume the peculiar virtue of our nation, to which they appeal. Ironically, they do not fail with equal consistency to commend any item of their foreign policy in terms that will appeal to the self-interest of the nation. The resulting moral confusion makes us rather uncomfortable allies, though it must be admitted that other nations have other, though equally efficacious, sources of national self-righteousness. Yet we have a particularly tough persistence of the illusion of the innocency of our nation, derived from the recency of our national childhood and our revolutionary beginnings. It is powerful enough to express itself in such diverse leaders as the late Woodrow Wilson and our present President, Dwight Eisenhower, and, more particularly, in his former Secretary of State, Mr. Dulles. The persistence of the illusion makes the confession of a Mexican philosopher pertinent. He declared: "You will scarcely understand how much patience is required to be the national neighbor of a nation which is at once so powerful and so innocent."

· · ·

The second point at which our public philosophy is defective is that we have no terms of reference that make the exercise of power above the level of the nation and blow the level of the universal community morally legitimate. We adhere strictly to the two dogmas of the foreign policy of the liberal democracy: the "self-determination of nations" and "collective security." The first dogma tempts us to make national autonomy into an inflexible principle of foreign policy, even if it should hurry the Netherlands unduly in granting independence to Indonesia after World War II and to interfere in the Middle East in the interest of the national autonomy of nations that may not, like Jordan, be capable of a viable national economy. It also impedes us from coming to terms with the total problem of the Middle East, where the supranational forces of an Islamic culture and of Arab "nationalism," so-called, outweigh the factors that support integral nationhood and open the way for Nasser's imperialism, posing as Arab nationalism.

The second item in the dogmatic presuppositions of liberal democracy is the principle of "collective security." It tempts us to regard the United Nations as a kind of supergovernment, rather than what it indeed is, a clearinghouse for international diplomacy. Our present administration was betrayed by this error into making common cause with Russia and the Arab-Asian bloc against Israel, Britain, and France. The President could lecture Israel on the duty of leaving the Gaza strip, after its victory over Egypt, in terms which assumed that the moral authority of the United Nations would alone insure peace; and the prerequisite of such moral authority was that no nation would ever resort to force to accomplish its ends.

In his television address on February 20, 1957, the President said: "When I talked on October last I pointed out that the United States fully realized that the military action against Egypt resulted from grave and repeated provocations; but I also said that the use of force to solve international disputes could not be reconciled with the principles and purposes of the charter to which we have all subscribed. I added that our country did not believe that recourse to force and war could for long serve the permanent interests of the attacking nations, France, Britain and Israel."

The President then paid tribute to the three attacking nations for obeying the resolution of the United Nations ordering them to quit the conquered territory "forthwith." He said this compliance made "a tremendous contribution to world order"; but he failed to say that they obeyed the United Nations simply because their closest ally, our own nation, made common cause with Russia in ordering them out. This was one of the few occasions in which the unanimity of the great powers, which the United Nations charter assumed to be the basis of world order, was in fact achieved. The absence of such unanimity made the United Nations something less than an organ of world order; and the idea that nations must obey the organization in order to increase its moral authority made confusion worse confounded. It perpetuated the quasi-pacifist illusions that informed Wilson's conception of the function of the League of Nations.

Nothing is more important in the reorientation of our public philosophy than that our nation recognize the importance of exercising responsibilities commensurate with its power, even though there are no precise constitutional forms for such exercise. The minimal constitutional form is that our policy conform to the general framework of the United Nations system. But the whole United Nations system of world order rested upon the implausible assumption that the great powers, which were allied in the defeat of Germany, would preserve their unanimity. Actually, the unanimity was not real during the war; and the divergent and even contradictory policies of the Soviet Union and the Western democracies became apparent immediately after the war.

It may have been inevitable that the general public should have continued to conceive of the functions of the United Nations in terms that were set by the euphoria of the postwar period, culminating in the San Francisco Conference and the founding of the United Nations. It was not so inevitable that political leaders should have been guided by these outmoded conceptions; but they were in fact so guided. In consequence, they wrongly believed that the United Nations made independent international policy to which we must conform. Actually, it was only an arena in which we, as the most powerful nation, were called upon to initiate policy. Our failure to do so in the Suez crisis gave Krishna Menon, the delegate from India, a brief hour of glory as the dominant force in the United Nations. A change in our public philosophy, which gives moral and political legitimacy to the exercise of our "imperial" power, despite the historic roots of our anti-imperialism, is a desperate necessity for our nation, to which both the academic and journalistic guides of the public conscience must contribute, and to which the journalistic guides have contributed rather more than the academic guides.

The final problem of orientating both the public and its leaders to the new international situation that has developed in the fifteen years since the end of World War II has to do with our conception of the foe or competitor, the communist system, with which we are locked in the fateful struggle of the cold war and with which we share the common predicament of possible involvement in a war of nuclear annihilation should either or both sides miscalculate the motives and purposes of the opposition or be seized by hysteria in the event of a significant defeat.

Though the system of international communism is informed by a seemingly inflexible dogma, it has become more flexible in adjusting itself to the ongoing currents of world politics than the supposedly more flexible system of an "open society" in the democratic world. That judgment is valid at least for our own nation, which, in defiance of the opinion of its European allies, still persists in regarding the triumph of communism in China as due to mistakes made by our State Department in the period in which Chinese nationalism gradually gave way to the power of Chinese communism, expressed in both military and political terms.

The changes in the communist world to which we must become adjusted, for the purpose both of competing with it and of coming to terms with it for the prevention of nuclear annihilation, could be enumerated as follows. 1) The development of technical efficiency has proceeded more rapidly than anyone expected, and the tempo has made our condescension toward Russia as a "backward country" a dangerous form of complacency. Russia's industrial production is growing at roughly the rate of 5 or 6 per cent per annum, compared with our 2-per-cent increase. Russia has the additional advantage of having lower consumer standards than our paradise of gadgets, so that its wealth can be more easily diverted to foreign-policy goals, whether these be defined as foreign aid to under-developed nations or the increase of the nuclear arsenal.

2) The Russian technical achievements include the competitive triumph over us in the field of rocketry or missiles. This triumph was first heralded by the Russian sputniks and was sealed in world opinion by the achievement of placing an artificial planet in orbit around the sun. It had sufficient fire power to defy the moon's gravitational field. The achievement was the source of tremendous prestige for Russia and might be said to have ended an era in which Western capitalism and democracy drew their prestige from the fact that they were regarded as the inevitable prerequisites of technical efficiency. The budding nations of Asia and Africa are more interested in technical and industrial competence than in democracy, which seemed at any rate beyond their immediate political competence, since it required Western civilization four centuries to make the fluid and multiple system of economic and political power compatible with both justice and stability. The Russian triumph would seem to give the communist system the same prestige of opening the gates to a technical civilization without the key of democracy, a key that was proved adequate in Western civilization only after four centuries of experimentation and under cultural and economic conditions that cannot be easily duplicated in the Orient.

3) The political methods of communism have changed radically without seriously altering the revolutionary dynamism with which its utopian creed is endowed. Instead

of preaching "revolution" to the "workers of the world,"
it is helping the nations and governments of the world to
achieve technical competence and national independence.
Thus, a creed designed for the desperate industrial workers
of the West, in the throes of the injustices of early indus-
trialism, has adjusted itself to the needs of the agrarian and
pastoral peoples of preindustrial communities. It uses its
anti-imperialism, combined with its credo that capitalism
and imperialism are intimately related, to tap the reservoir
of resentment which the nations of Asia and Africa have
against the Western nations, who dominated them in the
nineteenth century. The fact that this domination was
morally ambiguous rather than purely evil or "exploita-
tive," is, of course, carefully concealed in the communist
propaganda. It would in any case not be plausible to
budding nations who were more conscious of the arrogance
of their masters than of the benefits that those masters
conferred upon them, culturally, politically and economically. The anti-imperialism of the communist propaganda,
subordinate in the thought of Marx, and lifted into high
position by Lenin, has become the potent instrument of
communist prestige in the post-Stalin era. Ironically, the
cruel, enforced industrialization of Russia by Stalin's
despotism contributed to this prestige by making the
communist system the seeming source of both economic
abundance and national liberation.

4) The most important fact about our foes and com-
petitors, to which we must become adjusted if we would
share the world with them and prevent nuclear annihilation, is that despite the undemocratic form of its political
structure, and the consequent freedom of the oligarchy to
embark upon martial ventures, there is little reason to

believe that the Russians really want a war. Both official and public estimates of Russian purposes have drawn erroneous conclusions from faulty analogies with the Nazi dictatorship. Hitler needed war. Hitler was a dictator and could make war without the restraint of public opinion. *Ergo,* the Russians, being nondemocratic, also want and need war. So runs the mistaken analogy. The NATO conference as late as 1957 gave publicity to this charge and declared that communism sought world dominion by fair means or foul. The fact is that the communist system is too successful politically and economically to be tempted to military venture. Unlike Hitler, who had to succeed quickly by military means or perish, the communists have time on their side. They have a wide, rather than narrow, ground on which to stand.

The analogy with Nazism is, in short, almost totally erroneous and serves to perpetuate interpretations of the foe and competitor which obscure the fact that we are destined to wage decades of economic and political competition with him, if we are fortunate to escape the nuclear holocaust; and that if we should fall behind seriously in this competition, our desperation would be a greater temptation to begin the ultimate conflict than communist dogmatism.

This interpretation of the situation that confronts us does not exclude the possibility that the foe, having the ruthlessness of true fanaticism, might also exploit his present advantage over us in guided missiles, and might press us so hard as to create the danger of an ultimate conflict. In short, we must always face the two problems of competing with this competitor economically and in terms of the nuclear arsenal and of easing the tension of the cold war and accommodating ourselves to living in the same world with him. To do this successfully means the most tremendous task in rethinking both the basic philosophy which informs our attitudes and our conception of the purposes and methods of a competitor who has changed more rapidly than our ideas and preconceptions of him have changed.

No instrument of education has helped the American people more in this task of reorientation than the thoughtful journalistic media. It is worth recording that Walter Lippmann has crowned his years of political education of the American people with a memorable and influentially publicized interview with the Russian Premier, which emphasized the primary task of our competitive coexistence and its relation to our survival as a free civilization and our common survival with our foes in a shared world.

If the reaction of this admirer of Lippmann's service as a member of one of the democratic elite classes and an instructor of another elite group should be typical, rather than unique, among his many admirers and debtors, and if there should be a more general acceptance of his day-to-day reconstruction of the Public Philosophy of the nation than of the systematic effort to do so in the volume of that title, the conclusion might be warranted that it is more valid to reconstruct our political philosophy by pragmatic readjustments of the nation's vision of its perils and its responsibilities and by a systematic revision of its structure of government or its system of morals. Such a pragmatic revision would consist of a realistic account of our motives and ends in foreign policy and those of our adversaries, and insistence on modesty in making moral claims for our own position, and particularly the disavowal of complete disinterestedness as a nation. It would include an insistence on the necessity of both meeting the competitive threat of the adversary in every realm of national vitality, economic, political, and military; and on the necessity of agreements wherever opportunity is provided for reaching agreements which can be kept because they are mutually beneficial.

I take it that these are the main features in Lippmann's revision of our Public Philosophy, when he engages in the task pragmatically, rather than systematically. In pursuing that task, he has been one of the great educators preparing a young and powerful nation to assume responsibilities commensurate with its power and to exercise them without too much self-righteousness. He has thus helped a democracy to assume, rather than to abdicate, the tasks which democratic nations find difficult to fulfill because the available knowledge and historical perspective is always insufficient for the enormity of the problems encountered. Nevertheless, foreign policy conducted by an undemocratic elite remains an untenable alternative, proved to be even more inadequate.

XI

Walter Lippmann:
The Intellectual v. Politics

BY ARTHUR M. SCHLESINGER, JR.

At the depths of the Depression (if my memory is correct), the *New Yorker*'s "Talk of the Town," commenting on the reported formation of a Monarchist party in the United States, said that many Americans would be glad to settle for Walter Lippmann as king. Nor was this notion of the pundit as leader a novel one. At Harvard College nearly a quarter of a century before, Lippmann's classmate John Reed used to introduce him, not wholly satirically, as "Gentlemen, the future President of the United States!"[1] James Truslow Adams could recall discussing Lippmann in 1918 "with a distinguished American far from visionary in his judgments"; the forecast then was that Lippmann by forty might easily be governor of New York or Secretary of State.[2] Yet, for all such predictions, Lippmann through

---

[1] Granville Hicks, *John Reed* (New York, Macmillan, 1936), p. 34.
[2] J. T. Adams, "Walter Lippmann," *Saturday Review of Literature*, January 7, 1933.

his life has resolutely declined entangling political commitment; and his few brushes with operating responsibility seem only to have fortified this resolution. His career, in a sense, has been a long and troubled search to define the role of the intellectual in the polity of a free society.

His broad answer to this quest has been plain enough. The office of the intellectual, Lippmann has generally proposed, is to articulate the guiding faith which will enable society so to discipline itself and focus its purposes that its members can live effective, coherent, and fulfilled lives. To give the intellectual this function is to imply, of course, that such a central faith exists—that there is some ultimate perspective in terms of which everything else will fall into its proper place. Lippmann has believed this during most, though not all, of his life; and, in affirming the possibility of some sort of basic order and rationality in the universe, he has perhaps betrayed the fact that, of the two Harvard philosophers who influenced him most, one influenced him more profoundly than the other. Both George Santayana and William James greatly excited young Lippmann; but in the end, Santayana's realm of essences evidently struck deeper chords than James's radical empiricism. Lippmann used to say in later years that it was Santayana who saved him from becoming a pragmatist.[3]

Assuming, then, that there was a central something to articulate, that the apparent contrarieties of existence were somehow corrected and harmonized in a higher realm of essences, how would the intellectual best go about persuading the world to recognize its own rationality? The next question was the old and vexatious one of detachment

3 John Mason Brown, *Through These Men* (New York, Harper, 1956), p. 211.

v. commitment. Would the intellectual help most as a free individual or as part of a cause? by insisting on rigorous independence of mind or by entering and helping control the great practical movements of history? At Harvard, Santayana and James, wherever else they might disagree, agreed in viewing the world at a philosophic distance. Both were men informed by a critical and ironic tolerance of human diversity. Lippmann certainly shared this instinct for disengagement. Yet other forces of the day tugged at him. These were years of urgent social and intellectual ferment. The Progressive era was at high noon; and for a mind both sensitive and logical, the rampant humanitarianism and rationalism of the day argued against a course of total withdrawal.

It seems at first odd that a man of Lippmann's evident brilliance and promise appeared not to consider seriously the prospects of an academic career. He did stay on at Harvard for a year to serve as Santayana's assistant in a philosophy course; but from the start, he seems to have accepted a destiny as a commentator rather than as a professional philosopher. As a thinker deeply responsive to the complex equilibrium of intellectual forces around him, he chose the role of helping produce public sense in the community rather than pursuing private truth in individual solitude. His intelligence was, in the best sense, polemical rather than either technical or prophetic; his particular gift was the sensitive lucidity with which he reacted to the intellectual ebb and flow of his culture. From an early point, one can detect almost a contracyclical quality in his thought, as if he were impelled always to redress the balance against the dominating suppositions of the day—sometimes after he himself had given these suppositions their most clear and trenchant statement.

So, in 1911, for all the temptations of James and Santayana and Harvard philosophy, Lippmann must have felt some inadequacy in academic life. He worked afternoons in settlement houses; contact with Graham Wallas, at Harvard as visiting lecturer from the London School of Economics, enlarged his interest in social problems, even if Wallas himself was by then disenchanted with socialism; and his own dangerous susceptibility to syllogism doubtless beckoned him then, as it sometimes did later, toward deductive conclusions which very likely outstripped his practical beliefs. In any case, he called himself a socialist and became president of the Harvard Socialist Club; and, though his socialism never went very deep, it did go deep enough to involve him in his first experiment in political activism. For a few moments in college and after, socialism represented for him the transcendent faith through which the intellectual could crystallize the purposes and unify the energies of society. As he later ruefully remarked of this period, "The general scheme of the human future seemed fairly clear to me."[4]

His first job after finishing Harvard was to serve an apprenticeship in reporting to Lincoln Steffens on *Everybody's*. In 1911, George R. Lunn, running on the Socialist ticket, was elected mayor of Schenectady. Lunn soon invited the brilliant young Harvard socialist to join his staff, and Lippmann, with evident eagerness, seized the opportunity to serve the cause. The result was quickly disillusioning. "I have lived with politicians," Lippmann wrote sadly

[4] Walter Lippmann, *The Good Society* (Boston, Little, Brown, 1937), p. xi.

the next year. The good will of these municipal socialists was abundant, and their intentions were constructive. But the futilities of politics seemed unbearable. Petty vexations piled up into mountains; distracting details scattered the attention and broke up thinking; committee sessions wore out nerves by aimless drifting; constant speechmaking thrust men back on their weary stock of platitudes. "Misunderstanding and distortion dry up the imagination, make thought timid and expression flat, the atmosphere of publicity requires a mask which soon becomes the reality." His socialist colleagues used to claim that they were fighting "The Beast" or "Special Privilege." "But to me it always seemed that we were like Peer Gynt at struggling against the formless Boyg—invisible yet everywhere."[5]

Politics were obviously something more than the painless application by young intellectuals of general principles to concrete circumstances. Lippmann foresook Schenectady after a few months and, reflecting on the difficulties he had encountered, retired to Maine and wrote a perceptive and thoughtful book entitled *A Preface to Politics*. Here, in reformulating the political problem, Lippmann redefined his conception of the role in politics of the man of ideas. The essential political conflict, he felt, was between routine and creativity. The real business of statesmanship was not the preservation of order, the guarding of privilege, the administration of existing machinery; it was the anticipation of social wants, the invention of new forms, the preparation for new growths. "The deliberate making of issues," he wrote, "is very nearly the core of the states-

5 Walter Lippmann, *A Preface to Politics* (New York, Mitchell Kennerley, 1913), pp. 54-5, 183.

man's task. His greatest wisdom is required to select a policy that will fertilize the public mind."

But there were obstacles to the easy execution of this mission. One was the complexity of society. "It is a great question whether our intellects can grasp the subject. Are we perhaps like a child whose hand is too small to span an octave on the piano?" Yet, in the real world, Lippmann responded, action cannot always wait on thought; we must act on half-knowledge, illusion, and error, and trust to experience to convert mistakes into wisdom. An equal problem, it seemed, was the character of the public itself. If one trouble was lack of facts about society, the reason that newspapers and magazines would not print them, Lippmann contended, was less the pressure of advertisers than the awful sensibilities of readers.

No financial power is one-tenth so corrupting, so insidious, so hostile to originality and frank statement as the fear of the public which reads the magazine. For one item suppressed out of respect for a railroad or a bank, nine are rejected because of the prejudices of the public. This will anger the farmers, that will arouse the Catholics, another will shock the summer girl. Anybody can take a fling at poor old Mr. Rockefeller, but the great mass of average citizens (to which none of us belongs) must be left in undisturbed possession of its prejudices. In that subservience, and not in the meddling of Mr. Morgan, is the reason why American journalism is so flaccid, so repetitious and so dull.

How could these obstacles be overcome? How, given the complexity of the material on the one hand and the "prejudices of the public" on the other, could one make the issues that would replace routine by creativity? Lippmann's answer was, in effect, to propose a partnership between the intellectual, who could master the material, and the statesman, who could master the public. The intellectual would no longer intervene directly, as in Schenectady. Rather, the statesman would act as the intermediary between the experts and his constituency. The statesman, wrote Lippmann, instancing Theodore Roosevelt and the conservative movement, "makes social movements conscious of themselves, expresses their needs, gathers their power and then thrusts them behind the inventor and the technician in the task of actual achievement." With such creative leadership, "there will be much less use for lawyers and a great deal more for scientists." And more use also, he implied, for philosophers, for those who sought to make society conscious of its purposes and problems: "Make a blind struggle luminous, drag an unconscious impulse into the open day, see that men are aware of their necessities, and the future is in a measure controlled."[6]

In *Drift and Mastery* in 1914, Lippmann further clarified his notion of the intellectual's role in society's struggle for coherence. Civilization, he wrote, was, in effect, the "substitution of conscious intention for unconscious striving"—the constant effort "to introduce plan where there has been clash, and purpose into the jungles of disordered growth." But this process of mastery could no longer be haphazard and spasmodic. Nor was an emotional faith, like socialism, adequate to bring about control. "What men need in their specialties in order to enable them to cooperate is not alone a binding passion, but a common discipline." And this discipline lay at hand: it was science.

[6] *Ibid.*, pp. 26-7, 250, 105-6, 196-7, 301-2, 306-7, 315.

The discipline of science is the only one which gives any assurance that from the same set of facts men will come approximately to the same conclusion. And as the modern world can be civilized only by the effort of innumerable people we have a right to call science the discipline of democracy.

Drift and Mastery thus cast the intellectual as the articulator of the discipline of science in society's effort to control its own evolution. Lippmann did not mean by this, however, that the intellectual should detach himself from all purpose and striving. "If the student is merely disinterested," he wrote, "he is a pedant.... The true scientist is inspired by a vision without being the victim of it." What was necessary, as Lippmann put it, was not just ideas but "passionate ideas."[7]

He soon had an opportunity to test out his new conception of the relationship between the intellectual and politics. His argument in *Drift and Mastery* was the elaboration of a viewpoint which Theodore Roosevelt, borrowing a phrase from Herbert Croly, had baptized the "New Nationalism" three years before. In the course of 1914, Croly invited Lippmann to join him on the staff of a projected magazine to be called the *New Republic.* Croly had already provided in *The Promise of American Life* the best historical and philosophical vindication of Roosevelt's general ideas and attitude; and the *New Republic* promised to be, along with Roosevelt's own *Outlook,* the chief organ of Rooseveltian Progressivism. In November 1914, T. R. displayed his own high regard for Croly and Lippmann in an *Outlook* article on *Drift and Mastery* and Croly's new book, *Progressive Democracy:* "No man who

7 Walter Lippmann, *Drift and Mastery* (New York, Henry Holt, 1914), pp. 269, 281-2, 285, 307, 317.

wishes seriously to study our present social, industrial, and political life with the view of guiding his thought and action so as to work for National betterment in the future can afford not to read these books through and through and to ponder and digest them."[8]

The experiment in collaboration between intellectual and statesman seemed ideally conceived. And for a time everything went along swimmingly. "Our general position at the outset delighted Roosevelt," Lippmann later wrote, "and we saw a good deal of him in the first few weeks."[9] T. R. called Lippmann "a personal friend of mine ... I think, on the whole, the most brilliant young man of his age in all the United States. He is a great writer and economist. He has real international sense."[10] But events soon confronted Croly and Lippmann with the old choice between commitment and detachment—in this case between suppressing their opinion of a powerful friend in the hope of retaining their capacity to influence him, or publishing that opinion at the risk of estranging him. When Roosevelt launched a particularly crude attack on Wilson's Mexican policy, the *New Republic* preferred editorial integrity to personal loyalty, and condemned their patron. Roosevelt "reproached us bitterly," as Lippmann later recalled it, "and never forgave us." Lippmann added: "After that we never had any close personal association with any public man."[11]

8 Theodore Roosevelt, "Two Noteworthy Books on Democracy," *Outlook*, November 18, 1914.

9 Walter Lippmann, "Notes for a Biography," *New Republic*, July 16, 1930.

10 Theodore Roosevelt, *Letters* (Cambridge, Harvard University Press, 1954), Elting E. Morison, ed., Vol. VIII, p. 872.

11 Walter Lippmann, "Notes for a Biography."

This final statement undoubtedly expressed a moral which has ruled Lippmann ever since. A commentator could no more enjoy friendship with a statesman than a dramatic critic could with a leading lady. And this was true with T. R. despite an agreement on issues that persisted long after the personal coolness—which lasted, indeed, until, as Lippmann saw it, Roosevelt himself in 1916 deserted the New Nationalism and the philosophy of mastery in favor of a jumble of phrases about honor, patriotism, and righteousness. Up to this point, Lippmann had been critical of Wilson's New Freedom as the philosophy of drift, the vision of a nation of villagers. But gradually Wilson appeared to have apprehended the need for national purpose and control; the Democratic party, Lippmann concluded in 1916, was the "only party which at this moment is national in scope, liberal in purpose, and effective in action."[12]

If the experiments with Lunn and Roosevelt had destroyed for Lippmann the conception of the intellectual as close personal adviser, there still remained the essence of the role sketched in *Drift and Mastery*—the expert who could collaborate with the statesman in the task of social control. The *New Republic*'s rapprochement with Wilson now afforded an opportunity to explore the implications of this role. In the winter of 1916, Lippmann had two or three interviews with Wilson; and soon both he and Croly began to hold regular fortnightly meetings with Colonel House. Lippmann subsequently minimized the significance of this relation; any resemblance between the policies of the administration and the line of the *New*

12 A. M. Schlesinger, Jr., *The Crisis of the Old Order* (Boston, Houghton Mifflin, 1957), p. 35.

Republic, he said, was partly the result of "a certain parallelism of reasoning," partly of sheer coincidence.[13] Nonetheless, the relationship grew; and, when America entered the war, Lippmann, to Croly's dismay, took leave from the magazine and entered the government service.

There then ensued Lippmann's longest and most significant venture in official life. He first succeeded Felix Frankfurter as special assistant to Secretary of War Newton D. Baker, working particularly on labor matters (here, on an interdepartmental committee, he met Assistant Secretary of the Navy Franklin D. Roosevelt). Then, when House set up the Inquiry, a collection of experts to begin planning for the peace, Lippmann became its secretary and the chief liaison between the Inquiry and the White House. House's experts did the preliminary work on Wilson's peace proposals; and subsequently Lippmann himself, along with Frank Cobb, wrote what came to be accepted as the official American interpretation of the Fourteen Points.

In due course, Lippmann was commissioned in Military Intelligence and sent to France to pursue what another generation would call psychological warfare against Germany. Wilson was a little unhappy when he heard of this mission. "I have a high opinion of Lippmann," he wrote the Acting Secretary of War, "but I am very jealous in the matter of propaganda.... I want to keep the matter of publicity in my own hands."[14] But House continued to send Lippmann's reports to the President and eventually put Lippmann on his own staff in Paris.

[13] Walter Lippmann, "Notes for a Biography."
[14] R. S. Baker, *Woodrow Wilson, Life and Letters* (New York, Doubleday, 1939), vol. viii, pp. 384-5.

Peace making, however, turned out to be easier on paper than around a conference table. Lippmann, discouraged, resigned to return to the *New Republic* before the deed was finally done. There, with some misgiving, he accepted Croly's decision to oppose the result. His disillusion over Versailles was not so violent as that of some contemporaries; "if I had to do it all over again," he said in 1930, "I would take the other side."[15] Yet, on balance, he plainly felt that something had gone badly wrong, that his work had miscarried. Still, this failure did not invalidate his conception of the intellectual as the indispensable expert. It only challenged the way the intellectual's contribution was organized and the climate in which he worked. It was necessary now to go on beyond *Drift and Mastery* if the intellectual's role was to be adequately defined.

Why had Versailles failed? Lippmann's answer was that the people of Europe and America did not know the facts. Not knowing the facts, they were unable to protest the betrayal of ideals for which the war had been fought. Blocked by censorship and secrecy, they could not intervene to affect the negotiations at the time when intervention would have counted most and cost least. "In the last analysis," Lippmann wrote, "lack of information about the conference was the origin of its difficulties."[16] In *Liberty and the News* in 1920, he tried to draw out the implications of this proposition for the general theory of democracy.

Events in the United States meantime increased his concern about the adequacy of public information. The activ-

<hr>

15 Walter Lippmann, "Notes for a Biography."
16 Walter Lippmann, *Liberty and the News* (New York, Macmillan, 1920), p. 66.

ities of Attorney General A. Mitchell Palmer dramatized the power of the state to manipulate and suppress opinion. ("The most exhilarating experience we had, as I now look back," he wrote later, "was the resistance of the *New Republic* in 1919 and 1920 to the Red hysteria."[17]) The confusion of misinformation in even the New York *Times* concerning the Soviet Union showed the editorial irresponsibility of the press. Above all, Lippmann's increasingly oppressive sense of the complexity of modern society convinced him that if, on top of everything else, people were denied the facts, the common method of science could not hope to work, and men were doomed to bafflement and subservience. "There can be no liberty for a community which lacks the information by which to detect lies." It was necessary not only to have "a common intellectual method," but "a common area of valid fact" if the "unity of disciplined experiment" was to concert the hopes and energies of men. Freedom, in essence, meant the guarantee of the integrity of the sources of information. To assure the flow of uncontaminated fact, Lippmann proposed the establishment of technical research organizations which could help construct "a system of information increasingly independent of opinion." The intellectual, in short, should become the man, no longer of "passionate ideas," but of "neutral facts."[18]

Liberty and the News, for all its apprehensions about the actual workings of democracy, preserved the assumption that, given the neutral facts, the people as a whole could be relied on to act rationally. But Lippmann soon found he could not rest comfortably in this assump-

17 Walter Lippmann, "Notes for a Biography."
18 Walter Lippmann, *Liberty and the News*, pp. 64, 67, 91-2, 96-7, 99.

tion. As he gazed out at America in the twenties, he wondered if better reporting would really solve the problem
of public confusion and apathy. Was the "news" really
enough? Should he not have insisted more on a distinction
between "news" and "truth," the one registering an event,
the other expressing a vital relationship? With such
thoughts in mind, he turned anew to the whole question
of the popular psychology. The result, published in 1922
under the title *Public Opinion,* carried his argument still
another step away from his onetime faith in a rational
society.

Public Opinion is still a remarkable book. The stupefy-
ing mass of writing, both learned and popular, which has
appeared on this subject in the last quarter-century has
added surprisingly little to Lippmann's analysis; and none
of it has had anything like his fertility of insight or ele-
gance of expression. For most people, Lippmann argued,
the world they were supposed to deal with politically was
"out of reach, out of sight, out of mind." The real environment was replaced by a "pseudo-environment," compounded of ignorance, distortion, tradition, emotion,
stereotype, and manipulated consent.

These limitations upon our access to that [real] environment
combine with the obscurity and complexity of the facts themselves to thwart clearness and justice of perception, to substitute misleading fictions for workable ideas, and to deprive us
of adequate checks upon those who consciously strive to
mislead.

Public opinion, in consequence, became primarily "a
moralized and codified version of the facts." Nor would
liberation of the facts by itself affect a cure, since few

people were prepared to absorb them or to assess them at their proper significance. What was necessary was some means of making the facts intelligible, and this less for the people at large than for the few who had to make large decisions. Most people Lippmann felt obliged to dismiss as "outsiders," without the time, or attention, or interest, or equipment for judgment. It was the men on the inside, charged with power and responsibility, who made the decisions of society. And the role of the intellectual, Lippmann now believed, was precisely to serve these insiders. In a more urgent version of his research proposal of 1920, he called for bodies of experts, immune from the temptations of power, inspired by a "selfless equanimity," dedicated to the task of inventing and organizing a machinery of knowledge. These experts, Lippmann insisted, must confine themselves to the production of data for policymakers; they must themselves stay rigorously out of policy. "The power of the expert," as he put it, "depends upon separating himself from those who make the decisions, upon not caring, in his expert self, what decision is made." "The perfectly sound ideal," he added, in an odd forecast of the presidential philosophy of the nineteen fifties, "[is] an executive who sits before a flat-top desk, one sheet of typewritten paper before him, and decides on matters of policy presented in a form ready for his rejection or approval."[19]

Where the role of the intellectual had once been to declare the constitutional pattern of the universe to all mankind, now it was only to serve up neutral facts to the ruling elite. *Public Opinion* thus represented a further step

[19] Walter Lippmann, *Public Opinion* (Pelican ed.), pp. 271, 20, 56, 93, 41, 228, 280.

in Lippmann's disengagement of the intellectual from policies and values. And, as he ruminated over his distinction between insiders and outsiders, he found the role of the broad public increasingly shadowy and impalpable—a conclusion proclaimed in the title of his next book, *The Phantom Public,* in 1925. His growing skepticism about absolutes was carrying him into new positions—not, it should be emphasized, to a lack of faith in democracy, but to a lack of belief in any ultimate rationality behind it. Up to this point, he had clung to the supposition that the universe contained a pattern of meaning. Now for the first time he seemed to doubt whether there was any ultimate perspective in terms of which everything else would come into focus.

The private citizen, Lippmann began, was like the deaf spectator in the back row: "he does not know what is happening, why it is happening, what ought to happen"; "he lives in a world which he cannot see, does not understand and is unable to direct." Public opinion, in consequence, could not hope to deal with the substance of political issues. All it could do was to intervene in times of crisis to support one set of individuals or proposals against another. "Public opinion in its highest ideal will defend those who are prepared to act on their reason against the interrupting forces of those who merely assert their will."

In short, "actual governing is made up of a multitude of arrangements on specific questions by particular individuals"; public opinion was at best sporadically mobilizable to settle particular controversies. Santayana's realm of essences, where all conflicts would be reconciled and harmonized, was receding from view, leaving behind the

ARTHUR M. SCHLESINGER, JR.

prickly and unfinished universe of William James, filled
with an irreducible diversity of intractable and immiscible
facts and ideas. "The attempt to escape from particular
purpose into some universal purpose, from personality
into something impersonal," Lippmann now scorned as a
"flight from the human problem," though he added a
little wistfully, "It is at the same time a demonstration of
how we wish to see that problem solved. We seek an
adjustment, as perfect as possible, as untroubled as it was
before we were born." But man had moved beyond the
womb into the stubborn and inherent pluralism of reality.

Against this deep pluralism thinkers have argued in vain. They
have invented social organisms and national souls, and over-
souls, and collective souls; they have gone for hopeful analogies to the beehive and the anthill, to the solar system, to the
human body; they have gone to Hegel for higher unities and
to Rousseau for a general will in an effort to find some basis
of union.

All, all in vain. No such basis existed. Monism was a
delusion. We could no longer expect, Lippmann wrote,
"to find a unity which absorbs diversity. For us, the conflicts and differences are so real that we cannot deny them,
and, instead of looking for identity of purpose, we look
simply for an accommodation of purposes."[20]
    The Phantom Public was a brilliant and unrelenting
exercise in skepticism. At last, Lippmann despaired of finding the unifying vision he had pursued so long. By now
every universal pattern, every central perspective, seemed
to have washed out from under him: first, socialism; then

[20] Walter Lippmann, *The Phantom Public* (New York, Macmillan, 1925),
pp. 13-14, 39, 69, 41, 170-1, 97-8.

majority rule, derived from majority rationality; then the common method of science; then the common area of valid fact; then the provision of expert reports to insiders by disinterested social scientists. He had supposed that a fully informed people could govern modern society, but he had discovered, first, that the people were not fully informed, and, second, that, even if the facts were fully available, only a small minority were capable of absorbing them. The substantive unification of experience seemed an unattainable ideal. The hope he offered in *The Phantom Public* was procedural—agreement in the rules of the game, "the maintenance of a regime of rule, contract and custom," and, within that, the piecemeal resolution of pressing problems through the wisdom of statesmen and the knowledge of experts.[21]

One other hope remained; and here again he showed the impact of William James. Lippmann retained an emphasis on one factor in the equation as unpredictable and yet decisive—the human will. Logical analysis, Lippmann now said, might clarify the will and the situation in which it operated; but it could not, in the present state of the art, anticipate what the will would make of future situations in which it might find itself. "Until that time comes,—if it comes," Lippmann wrote, after due quotations from James,

—we shall lack the support and guidance of a philosophy. We shall live as we are now living without any sense of the whole, without any clear conception of our destiny, with only improvised ideas of what is the better and the worse.[22]

21 *Ibid.*, 105.
22 Walter Lippmann, *American Inquisitors* (New York, Macmillan, 1928), pp. 116-7.

This conclusion paradoxically prepared him for a resumption of the search for unity from a new tack. If objective ground for unity in human experience had given way under stress, the human will itself still remained as a source of moral energy. Could not man by an act of will instill in his own life a sense of order and coherence to replace the ancestral creeds now dissolving in the acids of modernity? This possibility provided the theme in 1929 for *A Preface to Morals*. If whirl was king, the key to intelligibility, Lippmann contended, lay within. It lay in man's capacity for "insight into the value of disinterestedness." Disinterestedness was the means of re-educating the passions which created the disorders and frustrations of life; it would render a dogmatic morality unnecessary; it would enable man to be harmonious with himself and with reality. Moreover, as he sought to show in detail, the ideal of disinterestedness had become "inherent and inevitable in the modern world." The discipline of science was one aspect; the growing importance in politics of "technicians, experts, and neutral investigators" was another. What the prophets had seen as the essence of high religion, what psychologists delineated as a matured personality, what society required for its practical fulfillment were, said Lippmann, "all of a piece and ... the basic elements of a modern morality." He sketched his portrait of the modern man:

The mature man would take the world as it comes, and within himself remain quite unperturbed. . . . Would he be hopeful? Not if to be hopeful was to expect the world to submit rather soon to his vanity. Would he be hopeless? Hope is an expectation of favors to come, and he would take his delights here and now. Since nothing gnawed at his vitals, neither doubt, nor ambition, nor frustration, nor fear, he would move easily through life. And so whether he saw the thing as comedy, or high tragedy, or plain farce, he would affirm that it is what it is, and that the wise man can enjoy it.[23]

The ideal of disinterestedness had been latent in his life-long faith that human reason could relieve the turmoils and unify the energies of society. Now, as everything else had crumbled away, it had become itself the means of salvation, man's only rock against the indifferent storms of a pluralistic universe. But the disinterested man was due for a testing sooner perhaps than Lippmann supposed. Shortly after *A Preface to Morals* came out, the Wall Street crash ushered in the long Depression. Abroad, totalitarian faiths won new converts and threatened new horrors. Did not now something begin to gnaw at the vitals of modern man? Could he move with such easy composure through a world now so demonstrably fearful and tragic?

Lippmann recognized the new pressures; but this recognition did not at first affect the ideal of disinterestedness. Speaking at the Columbia commencement in 1932, he mentioned the "special uneasiness" perturbing the scholar —"every student of economics and of politics, of law, of education, and of morals"—the feeling that he ought to be doing something about the world's troubles.

The world needs ideas: how can he sit silently in his study and with a good conscience go on with his thinking when there is so much that urgently needs to be done?

Yet, said Lippmann, the scholar also heard another voice, telling him that to do his job "he must preserve a quiet

23 Walter Lippmann, *A Preface to Morals* (New York, Macmillan, 1929), pp. 204, 208, 209, 231, 239, 271-2, 323, 329-30.

indifference to the immediate and a serene attachment to the processes of inquiry and understanding." The second voice was evidently Lippmann's own. If the scholar tried to make contributions to practical affairs, Lippmann warned, he might well "have less to contribute than many who have studied his subject far less than he"; worse than that, he would suffer in his own estimate when he pronounced conclusions in which he only half believed. What disqualified the scholar most of all was his inability to understand public opinion, with its transience, restlessness, and willfulness. "We must not expect society to be guided by its professors," Lippmann declared, "until, or perhaps I should say unless, the fluctuating opinions that now govern affairs are replaced by clear, by settled, moral values"—and this was the hope he had only recently dismissed as a fantasy of regression. What was most wrong with the world was that democracy had become the creature of the immediate moment. "With no authority above it, without religious, political, or moral convictions which control its opinions, it is without coherence and purpose. Democracy of this kind cannot last long. . . . But in the meanwhile the scholar will defend himself against it. He will build a wall against chaos." His duty above all was to refuse to let himself be absorbed by distractions about which, as a scholar, he could do nothing.[24]

Lippmann in 1932, while yearning for a settled moral pattern, for an order of authority above democracy, was thus still in his mood of *The Phantom Public* and *A Preface to Morals*; he evidently did not believe that that higher moral order, however desirable it might be, really

[24] Walter Lippmann, "The Scholar in a Troubled World," *Atlantic*, August, 1932.

existed. This faith in detachment as the strategy of pluralism persisted into 1933. What brought it to an end—what seems suddenly to have revived Lippmann's belief in ultimate patterns—was the explosion of moral and intellectual energy accompanying the first years of the New Deal.

Lippmann, who had now known Franklin Roosevelt for fifteen years, had watched his astonishing rise with a mixture of admiration and doubt. When Roosevelt received the vice-presidential nomination in 1920, Lippmann had wired him with enthusiasm: WHEN CYNICS ASK WHAT IS THE USE WE CAN ANSWER THAT WHEN PARTIES CAN PICK A MAN LIKE FRANK ROOSEVELT THERE IS A DECENT FUTURE IN POLITICS. Roosevelt's speech nominating Smith in 1924 stirred Lippmann to write a note praising it as "a moving and distinguished thing. I am utterly hard-boiled about speeches, but yours seems to me perfect in temper and manner and most eloquent in its effect." Lippmann's early respect had declined sharply, however, during Roosevelt's governorship. "The trouble with Franklin D. Roosevelt," he wrote during the Walker affair, "is that his mind is not very clear, his purposes are not simple, and his methods are not direct." In January 1932, he was provoked to his celebrated evaluation of Roosevelt as "not the dangerous enemy of anything . . . too eager to please . . . a pleasant man who, without any important qualifications for the office, would very much like to be President."[25] Nonetheless, when Roosevelt took over, Lippmann was generous in his praise of the new national leadership. "At the end of February," he wrote in a summary of Roosevelt's first Hundred Days, "we were a congeries of disor-

25 A. M. Schlesinger, Jr., *The Crisis of the Old Order*, pp. 362, 96, 395, 291.

derly panic-stricken mobs and factions. In the hundred days from March to June we became again an organized nation confident of our power to provide for our own security and to control our own destiny."[26]

If these were exciting days for Roosevelt, they were also exciting days for Lippmann. His vogue in 1933 was greater than ever before. James Truslow Adams called him "one of the most potent political forces in the nation ... the only national leader who has appeared in these post-war years."[27] More than this, he was having an impact on presidential decisions perhaps even greater than he had had fifteen years earlier. Roosevelt seems to have been a faithful reader of Lippmann, though apparently no effort was made on either side to resume close personal relations, and several moments can be isolated where Lippmann, by analyzing complex problems with lucidity, precipitated in Roosevelt's mind a solution toward which the President had, in his own more intuitive way, been groping.

Lippmann was particularly influential on monetary issues. Thus, when Roosevelt was pondering the question of the gold standard in the spring of 1933, a Lippmann column arguing that "a decision to maintain the gold parity of currency condemns the nation which makes that decision to the intolerable strain of falling prices" convinced the President that the gold standard would have to go. As Raymond Moley was departing for London and the World Economic Conference, Roosevelt sent him off with a quotation from Lippmann to the effect that international co-operation was a good idea if it resulted in concerted

26 A. M. Schlesinger, Jr., *The Coming of the New Deal* (Boston, Houghton Mifflin, 1959), p. 22.
27 J. T. Adams, "Walter Lippmann."

action, but not as an end in itself—not if it merely produced a negative and impotent stability. Lippmann himself was in London when Roosevelt's message to the
conference expressed his decision to give the American
price level priority over the stability of the international
exchanges. Not only did Lippmann defend the decision
publicly, but he collaborated privately with Moley and
John Maynard Keynes in drafting the official explanation
of the American position. Later, Lippmann urged tolerance toward the gold-purchase program, and in the spring
of 1934 his column provided the formula that broke the
deadlock over the congressional demand for silver-purchase
legislation.[28]

The excitement of watching intelligence at work in
public decision seems to have begun to restore Lippmann's
faith in the rationality of society. Perhaps this experience
could provide a pattern in which the disinterested man
could find a larger solace than Lippmann had offered him
in *A Preface to Morals*. "A planned society can exist," he
wrote, "only where disinterested men have the confidence
of the people"; and, while this state of beatitude was not
imminent, it represented, Lippmann believed, the direction in which society had to move. The unifying vision,
which he had renounced a few years before, was now
reappearing on the horizon. The "ideal of a consciously
controlled society" challenged man once again with a
transcendent purpose.

In our world, amid the wreckage of empires and the break-
down of established things, such a purpose has been born,

28 A. M. Schlesinger, Jr., *The Coming of the New Deal*, pp. 199-200,
216, 224-5, 241, 251.

and I say to you, my fellow students, that the purpose to make an ordered life on this planet can, if you embrace it and let it embrace you, carry you through the years triumphantly.

This ideal expressed, he thought, the revival of a deep instinct of men "for the unity of civilization." Taken as the animating principle of men's lives, it would offer "composure, purpose and confidence amidst the vast hurly-burly of modern things."[29]

Lippmann developed and refined this theme in his remarkable Godkin Lectures of 1934, published under the title *The Method of Freedom*. In some respects, this remains Lippmann's most brilliant and prophetic work. *Laissez faire,* he argued, had failed; the self-regulating and self-adjusting character of the old order had been destroyed; under modern conditions the state had no choice except to intervene. But it could intervene in two radically different ways. Here Lippmann distinguished between what he called the Directed Economy and the Compensated Economy. The Directed Economy was the centrally planned and physically regimented economy of the totalitarian state. The Compensated Economy, on the other hand, retained private initiative and decision so far as possible but committed the state to act when necessary to "redress the balance of private actions by compensating public actions"—by fiscal and monetary policy, by social insurance, by business regulation, by the establishment of minimum economic levels below which no member of the community should be allowed to fall.

Having stated the alternatives, Lippmann proceeded

[29] Walter Lippmann, *A New Social Order* (New York, John Day, 1933), pp. 16-17, 21-2, 24-5.

with precision to define the central political difficulty of the Compensated Economy.

> In substance, the state undertakes to counteract the mass errors of the individualist crowd by doing the opposite of what the crowd is doing: it saves when the crowd is spending too much; it borrows when the crowd is extravagant, and it spends when the crowd is afraid to spend . . . it becomes an employer when there is private unemployment, and it shuts down when there is work for all.

In short, the compensatory method required the state to act almost continually contrary to prevailing opinion. "Will a democracy authorize the government, which is its creature, to do the very opposite of what the majority at any time most wishes to do?" This was—and is—a searching question; it is no criticism of Lippmann to say that he failed in 1934 to answer it. In *The Method of Freedom,* he chose to speculate about institutional solutions to a problem which we would tend to regard today more a matter of education and leadership. But the book's whole argument implied a confidence in the human capacity to devise intelligent compensatory policies; it thereby enlarged and socialized the role of the intellectual.[30]

The next year, in *The New Imperative,* he reaffirmed his faith in the potentialities of rational planning. "If you wish to know why the political sciences are not [yet] a true discipline for the future guardians of our civilization, but are a haphazard collection of disconnected specialties," he explained, "this is the reason: it is disreputable to hold and to declare a positive and coherent conception of the

---

[30] Walter Lippmann, *The Method of Freedom* (New York, Macmillan, 1934), pp. 18, 46, 59, 74.

function of the state in a modern economy." It was "obscurantism," he continued, to say that society could not be governed without sacrificing personal liberties to the authority of the state; the only result of such talk would be to stop men from working on the problem that historic necessity compelled them to face.

We must answer the question that young men put to us. We must tell them that they will have to manage the social order. We must call them to the study, not warn them away from it, of how to achieve the healthy balance of a well ordered commonwealth.[31]

The sequel constitutes a puzzling passage in Lippmann's intellectual history. Toward the end of 1935, Lippmann began to lose his earlier confidence in Roosevelt's policies. For reasons not altogether clear, he began to see in the New Deal the unlovely lineaments of the Directed Economy. The paradox is that this impression began to seize his mind just at the time that the New Deal itself was shifting from the very policies Lippmann had identified in *The Method of Freedom* as measures of direction (like NRA and AAA) to the compensatory policies of public spending, social minima, and business regulation.[32] Perhaps it was that New Deal planning had failed in Lippmann's view to achieve the necessary qualities of impersonality and disinterestedness. Whatever the cause, Lippmann grew increasingly alarmed over what he considered a passion for centralization accompanied by ominous symptoms of arrogance and vindictiveness.

[31] Walter Lippmann, *The New Imperative* (New York, Macmillan, 1935), pp. 47, 51.
[32] Walter Lippmann, *The Method of Freedom*, p. 70.

In any case, in 1936, while retaining his revived faith in ultimate patterns, he abruptly recoiled from the expression of such patterns in social planning. "No greater delusion has ever cast its spell upon the human imagination," he wrote, "than that a group of mortal men can plan the future of a whole society and direct the affairs of a whole civilization." In a sharp reassertion of his old demand for absolute disinterestedness, he harshly condemned those college professors who had become "entangled in the making of policy and the administration of government."

It is only knowledge freely acquired that is disinterested. When, therefore, men whose profession it is to teach and to investigate become the makers of policy, become members of an administration in power, become politicians and leaders of causes, they are committed. Nothing they say can be relied upon as disinterested. Nothing they teach can be trusted as scientific. It is impossible to mix the pursuit of knowledge and the exercise of political power and those who have tried it turn out to be very bad politicians or they cease to be scholars.

"My own conviction," Lippmann concluded, "is that this choice has to be faced in American universities."[33] In a rare departure from his usual neutrality, he even called for the election to the presidency of Alf M. Landon.

Still, if planning were wrong, Lippmann had nonetheless re-embarked on his long quest for a unifying vision. The old ideal of individual disinterestedness was no longer enough by itself. It required a broader and solider foundation; it demanded a higher and more objective authority. In his language of 1932, the fluctuating opinions that gov-

[33] Walter Lippmann, "The Deepest Issue of Our Time," *Vital Speeches,* July 1, 1936.

erned affairs had to be replaced by clear and settled moral values if society were to be guided by its intellectuals. The search for a common moral discipline now replaced the common scientific discipline he had invoked twenty years before. The result was his book of 1937, *The Good Society*.

The Good Society is a curious and valuable work. It is curious because in so many respects it reads like a polemic launched by someone else against *The Method of Freedom*. In the earlier book, Lippmann had warned against those who would not distinguish "between the traditional policies of free states in the Nineteenth Century and the essentials of free government itself."[34] Now, under the influence of Hayek and von Mises—and perhaps, too, of Roosevelt's attack on the Supreme Court—Lippmann three years later seemed to verge on that error himself. Yet *The Good Society* remains valuable because in so many respects it restated the insights of *The Method of Freedom* in a different context. Though many took it at the time as a campaign document against the New Deal, Lippmann meant it primarily as a critique of fascism and communism; today it reads in great part as a vindication of the New Deal's essential idea.

At the beginning of *The Good Society*, Lippmann's earlier distinction between the Directed and the Compensated Economies appeared to vanish in a scatter-shot indictment of "nearly every effort which lays claim to being enlightened, humane and progressive" as involving "the premise of authoritarian collectivism." This indictment was launched in the name of liberalism, and liberalism, to the unwary reader of Lippmann (there were plenty in

[34] Walter Lippmann, *The Method of Freedom*, p. viii.

1937) appeared to be that same old idea of a self-adjusting, self-regulating economy whose obsolescence he had earlier demonstrated with such cogency. By proposing "graduated collectivism" as the intermediate stage on the road to perdition, by defining it as the resort to tariffs and bounties, price fixing and wage fixing, and other devices to supersede the sovereignty of the market, and by instancing the New Deal as a prime example, Lippmann further seemed to be rejecting the mixed economy in favor of the artificial resuscitation of classical liberalism. Yet the book contained, if it did not feature, unsparing criticism of latter-day liberals of the Spencer type; and actually, the Compensated Economy, having apparently been discarded at the start, was smuggled in later on in the book under the less provocative title of "The Agenda of Liberalism." This liberal agenda, with its plea for contracyclical spending, social insurance, antitrust action, collective bargaining, redistribution of income through taxation, and even the undistributed profits tax, adds up to a surprisingly accurate description of the policies of the New Deal of 1937 —the New Deal having, like Lippmann himself, for some time turned against the Directed Economy.[35]

Such implications of *The Good Society* were muted, however, because of the polemical orientation of the book —too many people read it as Lippmann's explanation of his vote for Landon. They were muted too because Lippmann, in his recoil against the illusion of the omniscient planner, seemed desperate to find an impersonal, automatic means by which society could regulate itself. He thus apotheosized the market and the law as self-operating tech-

35 Walter Lippmann, *The Good Society*, pp. 4, 119, 173, ch. xi.

niques of equilibration which could avoid the pitfalls of intervention by limited and fallible mortals. But these solutions were, of course, far less self-operative than they seemed on the surface. As his own text made clear, the market and the law were not automatisms at all; they were pseudoautomatisms: the market required supplementation and control, the law amendment and revision. Neither expressed the uncontaminated disinterestedness which he sought in the government of society. Both emerged from the conflicts, passions, and weaknesses of men. Far from guaranteeing unity in society, they only pushed the problem back a further step—to man himself.

Lippmann did not thus state the dilemma. But he evidently felt it, for *The Good Society* concluded with testimony about his dim but powerful apprehension of some law higher than parliaments, majorities, or kings. At this point, he could only define that higher law in procedural terms—as the denial that men may be arbitrary in human transactions. Yet he was ready to declare his intuition of the existence of some transcendent ethic, founded, not on the moral constitution of man, as in *A Preface to Morals,* but on the moral necessities of the universe. The search to define this ethic became his next intellectual preoccupation.

Lippmann began writing *The Public Philosophy* in 1938; it was finally published sixteen years later. Its argument was in curious counterpoint with that of *The Phantom Public,* taking off from a major conclusion of the earlier work but using that conclusion to justify a diametrically opposite philosophical result. In *The Phantom Public,* it is to be recalled, Lippmann's note of hope against the irreducible pluralism of the world was "the maintenance of a regime of rule, contract and custom." In 1925, this was for Lippmann a procedural conception. But in the years thereafter, what began as a functional necessity was somehow hypostatized into a transcendental faith—and then employed to abolish the very pluralism which had originally produced it. The invocation of due process grew into "a universal order on which all reasonable men were agreed," "a common conception of law and order which possesses a universal validity," natural law, the public philosophy. By this he meant the realm of essences ("I am using the ambiguous but irreplaceable word 'essence' as meaning the true and undistorted nature of things"), a world of "immaterial entities . . . not to be perceived by our senses," but nonetheless more real than anything else.

It was not someone's fancy, someone's prejudice, someone's wish or rationalization, a psychological experience and no more. It is there objectively, not subjectively. It can be discovered. It has to be obeyed.

In the name of the public philosophy, Lippmann spurned his pluralism of the twenties. A "large plural society," he argued, could not be governed "without recognizing that, transcending its plural interests, there is a rational order with a superior common law." This was so because it *had* to be so:

As the diversity of belief, opinion and interest became greater, the need for a common criterion and for common laws became more acute.... In this pluralized and fragmenting society a public philosophy with common and binding principles was more necessary than it had ever been.

And it was the responsibility of intellectuals to propagate the public philosophy. Even if they did, it might not be enough to save the West, Lippmann somberly wrote; but, "if the prevailing philosophers oppose this restoration and revival," the inexorable decline could not be arrested. In an unwontedly fierce statement from so normally courteous a man, Lippmann even suggested:

There is no reason to think that this condition of mind can be changed until it can be proved to the modern skeptic that there are certain principles which, when they have been demonstrated, only the willfully irrational can deny, that there are certain obligations binding on all men who are committed to a free society, and that only the willfully subversive can reject them.[36]

No one likes to nominate himself as willfully irrational or willfully subversive. Yet for those brought up in the tradition of James, Lippmann's conception of natural law, for all its nobility, cannot help seem an artificial construct.[37] Was he not succumbing to the very danger he warned against so eloquently a quarter of a century before —the "attempts to escape from particular purpose into some universal purpose, from personality into something impersonal"? Was this not, after all, the "flight from the human problem," the search for "an adjustment, as perfect as possible, as untroubled as it was before we were born"?

[36] Walter Lippmann, *The Public Philosophy* (Boston, Little, Brown, 1955), pp. 110, 104, 142.

[37] For searching philosophical criticism of Lippmann's argument for Natural Law, see Reinhold Niebuhr's essay in this volume, and also Morton White, *Social Thought in America* (rev. ed., Boston, Beacon, 1957), pp. 264-280. For an illuminating general discussion of the contrasting implications of the two theories (a) that all virtuous purposes are ultimately reconcilable (*The Public Philosophy*), and (b) that they are not (*The Phantom Public*), see Sir Isaiah Berlin's Oxford inaugural lecture, *Two Concepts of Liberty* (Oxford, Clarendon, 1959).

One wonders indeed whether so acute and honest a mind as Lippmann's can rest long in this solution. Are there perhaps signs that he is swinging back to a more vivid appreciation of the reality of pluralism? Certainly he was unsparing in his criticism when John Foster Dulles, almost as if in response to Lippmann's summons to the philosophers, sought to preach something sounding suspiciously like the public philosophy to our erring brothers overseas. In his most recent book, Lippmann appears to recede sharply from the notion that a single standard can comprehend the multifarious values and activities of the contemporary world. He condemns

the fallacy of assuming that this is one world and that the social order to which one belongs must either perish or become the universal order of mankind.

"The truth, as I see it," Lippmann now concludes, "is that there has never been one world, that there has never been a universal state or a universal religion."[38] One is tempted to ask: Has there ever been a public philosophy?

One can hardly criticize Walter Lippmann for having failed to clear up the problem of the One and the Many. Doubtless a few more years will go by before the great computers will end civilization's long suspense and break the problem down into its definitive mathematical solution. While the discussion lasts, one must be grateful for the urbanity and intelligence with which Lippmann through the years has pursued in his own mind the long

[38] Walter Lippmann, *The Communist World and Ours* (Boston, Little, Brown, 1959), pp. 50-1.

dialogue set off by James and Santayana at Harvard half a century ago.

As Lippmann has followed out his explorations, he has envisaged a number of roles for the intellectual, though most often as the disinterested voice of some unifying vision, from socialism through science to the public philosophy. For a season in the twenties, the unifying vision disappeared from view; but the urgencies of a collapsing world brought it back. For Lippmann, the intellectual has been most characteristically engaged in ideas, disengaged from movements; he is something different from the man who makes decisions and does things; his responsibility remains always somehow to influence the actor and permeate the culture. One cannot be sure, though, whether he speaks for the public philosophy or for himself.

If Lippmann has not really solved the role of the intellectual in free society, it must be said that he has magnificently exemplified it. In *Public Opinion,* he recounts the scene in Book V of *The Republic* when Socrates stalks out after warning Adeimanthis to attribute the uselessness of philosophers "to the fault of those who will not use them, and not to themselves." Lippmann comments: "Thus, in the first great encounter between reason and politics, the strategy of reason was to retire in anger."[39] As the veteran of many such encounters, Lippmann has rarely taken the easy course of withdrawal into irresponsibility. "We are challenged, every one of us," he wrote as a young man, "to think our way out of the terrors amidst which we live."[40] He has not flinched from that challenge. His man-

[39] Walter Lippmann, *Public Opinion,* p. 311.
[40] Walter Lippmann, *The Stakes of Diplomacy* (New York, Henry Holt, 1915), p. 10.

ner of meeting it has been a credit to himself and often a salvation to his contemporaries.

He once spoke of the Compensated Economy; he is himself a wonderful example of the Compensated Mind, seeking through continuous intervention to restore our society to the paths of decency and rationality. When the crowd has boasted a common faith, as in the twenties, Lippmann has stressed pluralism; when the crowd appears to have no faith at all, as in the fifties, he stresses monism (except as against the too insistent faith of Mr. Dulles, when he again turns to pluralism); when the crowd is overcommitted to drift, he stresses mastery; when the crowd is overcommitted to mastery, he stresses drift. The classic clarity of his language, studded, it would seem, with lapidary absolutes, has obscured the almost tactile sensitivity of his mind. His commentary has probed the problems of society and the problems of philosophy with unfailing reason and grace. He has preserved a fine magnanimity of temper in rancorous times and against bitterly unfair innuendoes and attack. His spirit has been both independent and compassionate.

Above all, Lippmann has insisted in the heat and clamors of the present on the indispensability of the long view. He once wrote,

This is not the last crisis in human affairs. The world will go on somehow, and more crises will follow. It will go on best, however, if among us there are men who have stood apart, who refused to be anxious or too much concerned, who were cool and inquiring and had their eyes on a longer past and a longer future.

By their example they can remind us that the passing

moment is only a moment; by their loyalty they will have cherished those things which only the disinterested mind can use.[41]

If this is the intellectual's responsibility, then Walter Lippmann has discharged it superbly; and his age stands deeply in his debt.

[41] Walter Lippmann, "The Scholar in a Troubled World."

XII

Conclusion: The Mockingbird and the Taxicab

BY JAMES RESTON

Walter Lippmann lives in the old former deanery of the Washington Cathedral at 36th Street and Woodley Road. He works in a second-floor study that looks out on the towering north transept of the Cathedral. Books and newspapers surround him. Over his desk are steel engravings of the Right Honorable Charles James Fox and the Right Honorable William Pitt, and between Pitt and Fox is a line drawing of James Thurber's man and woman, with the latter saying: "Lippmann Scares Me This Morning."

It is an appropriate setting: part intellectual, part political, with shadows of the spiritual in the background. It is quiet and orderly. Even his chimney is padded to muffle the melodic repertoire of a noisy mockingbird which he doesn't want to disturb and doesn't want to hear. But every Monday and Wednesday, precisely at 12:30 P.M., a Yellow taxicab from the Washington *Post* pulls up to his 36th Street door for his column. Later, at exactly 1:15, Miss

Charlotte Wallace and Miss Jean Wehner, one reading and the other checking, telephone the column to Miss Bertha Rees at the New York *Herald Tribune,* and he emerges from the cloister to the clamorous world of Washington politics and journalism.

This has been the orderly method of Walter Lippmann for over forty years: half in the noisy pit and half in the quiet study, a duality of engagement in the world of public affairs and disengagement from the world of affairs into the world of books and political philosophy, of reason and meditation on ultimate values. He writes in *The Public Philosophy* about "The Two Realms." These are the realms of heaven and earth: "that of this world where the human condition is to be born, to live, to struggle and to die; and that of the transcendent world in which men's souls can be regenerate and at peace." He himself has lived in these two realms, but mainly he has dwelt in two parts of the realm of the earth: in the theoretical realm of the ideal society and in the more practical and mundane realm of day-to-day political problems.

"I have lived two lives," he said recently. "One of books and one of newspapers. Each helps the other. The philosophy is the context in which I write my columns. The column is the laboratory or clinic in which I test the philosophy and keep it from becoming too abstract."

The remarkable thing about Walter Lippmann is that he has lived these two lives simultaneously, that he planned it that way two generations ago, and that he is still going at it with extraordinary physical and mental vigor at seventy.

As early as 1922, he placed on the title page of his book

Public Opinion, a quotation from Book VII of *The Republic* of Plato:

Behold! human beings living in a sort of underground den ... they have been here from their childhood and have their legs and necks chained so that they cannot move, and can only see before them. ... At a distance above and behind them the light of a fire is blazing. ... This is a strange image ... and they are strange prisoners ... they see only their own shadows, or the shadows of one another, which the fire throws on the opposite wall of the cave.

Even then, Lippmann was clearly trying to turn men's eyes from the flickering shadows on the wall of the cave to the brighter and larger world outside. He was in the cave of shadows, the world of newspapers, but pointing to the light, the better world, outside. When he later had to name his column, he called it "Today and Tomorrow," again symbolizing the two worlds of the cave and the universe, and it explains why he has consciously lived as he has.

He could have lived the academic life at Harvard or Chicago or any number of other places, but this would have limited his participation in the lively world of political decision. He could have lived the life of a government official, but this would have chained him in the cave and violated his concept of disinterestedness, of nonattachment to governments or parties or specific policies, and thus limited his pursuit of the ideal society. And while he flirted briefly with both the university and government lives, he made his choice fairly early.

At eighteen, he wrote a review of a book (*The Privileged Classes*) by a Harvard English professor, Barrett Wendell, in the *Harvard Advocate*. When the review appeared, William James, who was then retired but living in Cambridge, walked across the Harvard Yard to Lippmann's room in Weld Hall and praised his spirit and writing. Thereafter, James inspired Lippmann, in a series of Saturday-morning conversations at James's house on Irving Street, to continue writing on political and philosophical subjects.

Lippmann did not hesitate long in rejecting the academic life as the means to this end. He took his degree at Harvard in three years and was just about to take the examinations for his master's degree when a new magazine, the Boston *Common,* was started. He passed up the degree to join the magazine.

No doubt Walter Lippmann, at seventy, would prefer to be judged on his books of political philosophy, on the ground of his two mentors, George Santayana and William James. Even now he says, "James was the hero of my life." But while philosophy may be his love, journalism has been his mistress, and the amazing thing is that he has managed to be so faithful to both.

This has been done by applying to himself what he is always advocating for governments: a plan of action, a clearly thought-out set of priorities, a disciplined procedure that prevents secondary things from impinging upon primary things, and time for thought.

Governments may not follow Walter Lippmann's advice, but he follows it himself and it has not been easy. Few Washington newspapermen, even those who analyze rather than gather the news, ever manage to reconcile their professional and private lives. They are the playthings of events. Just when they are in the midst of a paragraph, the ticker summons them to some conference or pronouncement, or somebody pops into the room with the latest political idiocy, and they take time out to run or listen.

Lippmann himself once described part of this life in a lovely vignette on Mr. Justice Holmes's seventy-fifth birthday, in 1916:

The country's business at Washington is conducted in an odor of dead and dying cigars suspended in steam-heat. Out-of-doors Washington is widely planned and men might move about it thinking for a nation. But in the halls of Congress, in the committee rooms, the air is warm and foul.

It drags upon you till you wilt and your head swims, and the faces of men testifying grow hazy. In that mean atmosphere, so like the corridor of a cheap hotel, there is an invitation to relax and grow bored and cease to care. . . .

But there is at least one place in Washington where things have an altogether different quality, and no one, I think, comes away from it unmoved. . . .

Thereupon, he described the house of Holmes, whose "heart is with the laughing sad men." But he might have been contrasting the atmosphere and procedure of Washington today with the atmosphere and procedure of his own life.

Walter Lippmann is at least one newspaperman who gets home for dinner. His life is not commanded by events. It is a lively enough life, but it is lively in the way and with the people he and his wife want it to be. He guards and spends his time as a shrewd investor guards and spends his money. He is up to the minute with the news but he keeps his news ticker and his television in a closet, to be used like a broom or a razor for a specific limited purpose. As a result, he is almost the only thoughtful man

I know in Washington who never complains that he cannot find time to think.

At the beginning of a day, or a week, he knows precisely what he is going to be doing in that period. More surprising, if you ask him on New Year's Eve what he is going to be doing in the coming year, the chances are that he has a fairly detailed plan worked out. He knew at the beginning of this year, for example, that he was going to Europe on February 28; getting back on March 29; leaving for his Maine camp on June 7; returning September 9; and going to Europe again in October.

One day last March, the ticker announced that the Big Four foreign ministers' meeting would be held in Geneva on May 11, and all the rest of us started booking our reservations, scattering our kids, and changing our private and professional plans to be there, but not Lippmann. He carried on with his normal program, which did not include Geneva.

This is typical. Consider the preparation of his column. He may meditate on it for days and fix his calipers between the State Department and the distant stars, but he writes it by the ticking of the clock. Mockingbird or no, the taxi is arriving at 12:30 and the long-distance call is going through to the *Herald Tribune* at 1:15.

At nine o'clock, breakfast out of the way, the New York *Times*, the New York *Herald Tribune*, and the Washington *Post* read, he sits down at his desk with pencil and bond paper, and the count-down starts. He cannot stop the buses in Woodley Road, and the telephones may ring softly in the 36th Street side of the house, but on *his* side nothing is allowed to interfere with his task.

Nobody knocks on the door or runs the sweeper or ham-

mers up a screen door for the next two-and-a-half hours.
If his two assistants, his research aide and his secretary,
walk around, they must have on their gum-soled shoes, and
if he doesn't emerge by 11:45, everybody in the house
begins to wonder.

Such, however, is his concentration and discipline of
mind that usually around 11:15 his voice is heard. This is
a sign that he has finished writing and is dictating the
column from his own tidy handwriting into the Dicta-
phone. In the process, he will edit the prose occasionally
to improve the cadence or substitute a more vivid or simple word, and then an original and two copies are typed
with wide margins. One is given to his research assistant—
either Barbara Donald or Frances Van Schaick—to check.
He reads over, and may change, the other, and after a brief
conference with the researcher, it is retyped, checked again,
and ready for the 12:30 messenger.

Only when he finishes writing will he look at the morning mail. While the column is being typed, he will dictate
or write answers in reply, and shortly after 12:30, he will
be dressed and off downtown to the Metropolitan Club
for lunch, usually with a newspaper colleague or diplomat
or official.

After lunch, he drives himself back home (he never
drives after dark), and devotes most of the rest of the afternoon to recreation. If it is a good day, he and his wife,
Helen, will drive up the Canal towpath by the Potomac,
let the dogs out and walk for an hour. Or they may golf
at the Army-Navy Country Club, or, if it is bad weather,
go to the movies.

Between 4:30 and 6:00, he has a rest, reads the foreign
newspapers, makes notes of ideas for future columns, then

usually goes out to dinner with friends in the embassies or the government, or entertains at home.

This reflective and disciplined life has given his writing a scope and grace unmatched in American journalism today and probably not surpassed by any living political writer in the English language. His personal experience in government goes back to the days of Woodrow Wilson in World War I and the years just before the war. He has steeped himself in the history of his country and its relations with the world. He has studied the great political philosophers. He has access to the best minds in the Western world, and has patiently written his political philosophy in a series of books that stretch over almost fifty years and still retain much that is fresh and useful today.

Nevertheless, I see him first, not as an original philosopher, but as a man and a newspaperman. He is a gentle person in the best sense of that term: extremely sensitive, easily hurt, even by noise, loathe to criticize anybody who does not have the means of counter-criticism: in short, the antithesis of what is widely regarded as the typical newspaper extrovert.

There is nothing more hazardous than trying to analyze a man who spends his life analyzing others, but what impresses me is that, before he analyzed others, he analyzed himself, and not only had the imagination to select a useful and high-minded life, but the discipline and ability to live it in the noisy world of politics and newspapers.

Matthew Arnold made two comments about criticism almost a hundred years ago that summarize what I believe to be Walter Lippmann's special contribution to his time. He said (in "The Function of Criticism at Present Time") that Edmund Burke was great because "he brings thought

to bear on politics, he saturates politics with thought. . . .
His greatness is that he lived in a world which neither
English Liberalism nor English Toryism is apt to enter:
the world of ideas, not the world of catchwords and party
habits. . . ."

This is true of Walter Lippmann, but what is more
important, I believe, is that he has spent most of his life
performing this function of criticism, not in philosophic
tracts for the few, but in newspapers and periodicals which
reached a wide audience. And he did it, first in a period
of national contraction during the twenties, and second in
a period of revolutionary expansion of American influence,
when old habits of thought and political action were in the
process of unusual change.

Again Matthew Arnold defines this special role in his
essay "Sweetness and Light" (1867):

The great men of culture are those who have a passion for
diffusing, for making prevail, for carrying from one end of
society to the other, the best knowledge, the best ideas of their
time; who have labored to divest knowledge of all that was . . .
abstract, professional, exclusive; to humanize it, to make it
efficient outside the clique of the cultivated and learned. . . .

This is what Walter Lippmann has done; he has brought
thought to bear on politics, and he has carried that thought
from one end of our society to the other.

His critics, of whom there are many, say that he was
wrong in his early estimates of Franklin D. Roosevelt, and
Adolf Hitler, and John Foster Dulles, and many others;
that he is better at analyzing a problem than finding a
practical solution to it; that he has even violated his own
ideal of "disinterestedness," as in his support of Landon

234

in 1936 when he was feuding with Roosevelt; and that he made appalling miscalculations about America in the thirties and Germany in the forties and fifties.

Maybe so. The point is not that he was never wrong or that he did not change his ideas and even on occasion contradict his own theories, but that he provoked thought, encouraged debate, forced definition, and often revision, of policies, and nourished the national dialogue on great subjects for over half a century.

It is not easy—sometimes, indeed, it is presumptuous and even preposterous—to indulge in quick clinical analysis of speeding and complicated events to meet a newspaper deadline. Space as well as time is a problem, and while the human mind "hungers and thirsts after explanation," the effort to reduce diversity to identity often results in excessive simplification.

Therefore, even though Lippmann seldom employs blunt instruments and never tries, like Mencken, to "rattle his opponent's back teeth," he often annoys the policy makers even when he is addressing their reason. For, while they respect his experience and admire his style and clarity, they are constantly complaining, as one of them remarked, that "he is often clearer than the truth."

Nevertheless, it is precisely because he is their most experienced and learned critic, and because he is read so avidly by the political opposition and the learned community of the nation, that he commands their attention and is singled out for official complaint.

He annoys them, too, because, unlike Matthew Arnold, who thought "disinterested" criticism should "leave alone all questions of practical consequences and applications," Lippmann feels a moral duty to deal with the practical consequences, to parallel what he has criticized with his own alternative.

This sometimes leads him to propose solutions when even the men he admires the most in government life think the situation calls for "a little judicious leaving alone." Also, he occasionally seems to be searching for a *different* solution from everybody else's, as though, like other newspapermen who are forever seeking information "scoops," he felt obliged to come up with an "intellectual scoop." Nevertheless, he rejects the view that it is enough to analyze a problem.

"It is not enough to criticize the official's policy," he says. "We must put ourselves inside his skin, for unless we have tried to face up to the facts before him, what we produce is nothing but holier-than-thou moralizing."

This is Lippmann, the young aide to Elihu Root and Colonel House, talking. He has grafted onto the philosopher not only the journalist but the diplomat, and this explains another source of criticism against him.

Lippmann, the philosopher, would no doubt say that the forced division of Germany by the Red Army fourteen years after the armistice of 1945 is a wicked injustice. But Lippmann, the statesman, putting himself inside his friend Christian A. Herter's skin, sets himself a different problem: not the philosopher's problem of right and wrong, but the statesman's problem of how to get out of the mess.

To talk of war as a rational instrument of foreign policy when the destructive capacities of war now exceed any rational purpose seems to him a kind of madness—a particularly ominous shadow on the wall of Plato's cave. So his reason compels him to propose accommodations, which his critics condemn as appeasement.

They condemn him, of course, because nations do not live by reason alone—otherwise reason would have forbidden the American revolution or the British decision to carry on the war after Hitler's conquest of all Western Europe. But nations do not endure, either, by ignoring reason in an era of atomic weapons, and it is part of his achievement that Walter Lippmann does have the power to compel debate between reason and instinct.

It is not that Mr. Herter—or Mr. Dulles, or Mr. Acheson before him—is suddenly transported into new visions of truth by reading Lippmann at the breakfast table and rushes forthwith to the State Department to mend his ways. More often than not, the Secretary of State is more annoyed than persuaded, but the point is that other powerful men in the Congress or the press or the universities—and some down at the pick-and-shovel level of the State Department—probably were persuaded, and introduced Lippmann's ideas into the policy debate.

The curse of the average contemporary newspaper column, or, as Lippmann prefers to call it, "signed editorial," is that it sounds like a stuck whistle. Most columnists never surprise you. Each day's news is either a dreary and undistinguished report of the obvious or merely a new peg for the old tired themes. But not Lippmann.

He always has something to say. He has an unusual gift of cutting through the underbrush, and while he does not try to write in the vernacular—he rather deplores it—he uses the English language as it should be used.

When he returned not so long ago from Russia and later from Germany, his reports were part of the common conversation of the Capital. Every embassy up and down Sixteenth Street and Massachusetts Avenue discussed them and reported them to their governments. Members of the Senate Foreign Relations Committee read them and questioned the Secretary of State on his points. This is his multiplier quality that is so important.

Also, through the medium of the daily newspaper, he manages to address a vast audience while it is paying attention. The readers of his books on political philosophy are numbered in the thousands, the readers of his column in the millions. He talks to them when some particularly compelling headline has startled them out of their normal preoccupation with family or professional life. This is an act of public education which few writers ever equal.

Others are better qualified than I to make an estimate of his philosophical contributions, but I know that he has given my generation of newspapermen a wider vision of our duty. He has shown us how to put the event of the day in its proper relationship to the history of yesterday and the dream of tomorrow.

It is a delight to pay tribute to him and to express, while he is still showing us the way, at least a small part of the esteem in which he is held by his colleagues.

Index

* Indicates books and articles by Walter Lippmann